THOMAS MANN

TWAYNE'S WORLD AUTHORS SERIES

A Survey of the World's Literature

Sylvia E. Bowman, Indiana University

GENERAL EDITOR

GERMANY

Ulrich Weisstein, Indiana University

EDITOR

Thomas Mann

(TWAS 47)

TWAYNE'S WORLD AUTHORS SERIES (TWAS)

The purpose of TWAS is to survey the major writers —novelists, dramatists, historians, poets, philosophers, and critics—of the nations of the world. Among the national literatures covered are those of Australia, Canada, China, Eastern Europe, France, Germany, Greece, India, Italy, Japan, Latin America, New Zealand, Poland, Russia, Scandinavia, Spain, and the African nations, as well as Hebrew, Yiddish, and Latin Classical literatures. This survey is complemented by Twayne's United States Authors Series and English Authors Series

The intent of each volume in these series is to present a critical-analytical study of the works of the writer; to include biographical and historical material that may be necessary for understanding, appreciation, and critical appraisal of the writer; and to present all material in clear, concise English—but not to vitiate the scholarly content of the work by doing so.

Thomas Mann

By IGNACE FEUERLICHT

State University College, New Paltz

Twayne Publishers, Inc.   ::   New York

12-17-69

Library of Congress Catalog Card Number: 68-24312

For my sister Natalie

Preface

Thomas Mann is the most representative German author of the twentieth century. More honors have been bestowed on him than on any other writer, and perhaps more books and articles have been written about him than about any other modern author. He is famous in Europe and the United States, in Japan and Latin America. Since his death in 1955, literary scholarship concerning his work has further increased, thanks partly to the Thomas Mann Archive in Zurich and to the publication of many of his letters as well as his "collected works." Several periodicals have published special Thomas Mann issues, several anthologies of articles about him are now in print, colleges offer special courses on him, and in many countries his books and stories have become recommended or required class readings. No other German writer of our time—neither Hesse, or Rilke, or Musil, or Brecht, nor even Kafka—has been read as widely and consistently as Mann. The announced publication of his notebooks and diaries will only give new impetus to the general interest in his work.

This book intends to be a critical introduction to Mann's challenging and rewarding works. The plots and the ideas contained in his novels and stories, as well as the characters and the style, will be analyzed against the background of the author's life. I have gratefully utilized the findings of many critics and added my own observations and formulations, some of which are developed in more detail in my German book, *Thomas Mann und die Grenzen des Ich,* published in Heidelberg. This study is not centered on "ideas" or "problems," as some other publications about Mann are, but on the works themselves. That is why nearly every chapter is concerned with only a single work.

Because of the enormous literature on Mann, only a selected number of secondary sources could be listed in the bibliography.

Whenever an article has later been included in a book, it is not listed separately. No definitive biography or critical study of Mann has yet appeared in any language. The bibliography of Klaus Jonas, a second volume of which was published recently, is a ready and reliable guide to Thomas Mann research.

The page numbers in parentheses refer to first English editions, which are listed in the bibliography, except for *The Magic Mountain* and *Joseph,* where they refer to the one-volume editions. The page numbers in the stories refer to *Stories of Three Decades.* I am grateful to Alfred A. Knopf, Inc., the American publishers of the work of Thomas Mann, and to Secker and Warburg, Ltd., its publishers in the English Commonwealth, for permission to quote from their copyrighted editions of Mann's works. In some instances, I had to change or correct the translation or note omissions, for it is impossible for any translator to do full justice to Mann's stylistic variety, complexity, subtlety, and allusiveness.

I am also grateful to Erika Mann and the German Information Center for their kind permission to use Thomas Mann's photograph. It shows the author in his seventieth year.

Contents

THOMAS MANN

by

IGNACE FEUERLICHT

This book is intended to be an introduction to Thomas Mann's novels and stories. Thomas Mann, one of the great novelists of all times, is the most representative German author of the twentieth century.

Mann's esthetic and political ideas, his narrative technique, his mythology and psychology, his dazzling style, his superb humor, and his subtle irony are analyzed and interpreted. His relationships to great writers such as Goethe, Schiller, Novalis, Schopenhauer, Wagner, Nietzsche, Freud, and Proust are critically presented. A gallery of burghers and princes, writers and composers, cranks and cheats, saints and sinners, lovers and patriarchs, women and children are viewed in a new and revealing light.

In each chapter of this study, only one work by Mann is discussed. "Death in Venice" and *The Magic Mountain,* favorite readings in the United States, are given detailed interpretations.

Chronology

1875   Born in Lübeck on June 6, the second son of the merchant and senator, Johann Heinrich Mann.
1892   Death of father, liquidation of firm.
1893   Moves to Munich.
1894   Works in a fire insurance company.
1896–
1898   Lives in Italy (Rome, Palestrina).
1897   Begins *Buddenbrooks*.
1898–
1899   Works for the satiric magazine *Simplicissimus*.
1898   *Der kleine Herr Friedemann*, a collection of novellas.
1901   *Buddenbrooks*.
1903   *Tristan*, a collection of novellas, including "Tonio Kröger".
1905   Marries Katja Pringsheim.
1909   *Königliche Hoheit*.
1912   *Der Tod in Venedig*.
1918   *Betrachtungen eines Unpolitischen*.
1924   *Der Zauberberg*.
1929   Awarded the Nobel Prize.
1930   *Mario und der Zauberer*.
1933–
1938   Stays in Switzerland.
1933–
1943   *Joseph und seine Brüder*.
1938   Moves to the United States; lecturer at Princeton.
1939   *Lotte in Weimar*.
1940   Moves to California. 1942-1952 lives in Pacific Palisades.
1944   Becomes an American citizen.
1947   *Doktor Faustus*.
1951   *Der Erwählte*.
1952   Returns to Europe; lives near Zurich.
1953   *Die Betrogene*.
1954   *Bekenntnisse des Hochstaplers Felix Krull*.
1955   Dies in Zurich of thrombosis, August 12.

CHAPTER 1

The Decline and Fall of a Family

1901 was an important year in the history of the novel. For in October of that year *Buddenbrooks,* a novel in two volumes, by Thomas Mann, who was twenty-six years old and practically unknown, was published in Berlin by S. Fischer. In the spring of 1897, the publisher had urged Mann, who until then had written only a few stories, to try his talent on a larger piece of fiction. Work on *Buddenbrooks* began in October, 1897, and was finished in May, 1900. Mann's first novel was concerned with the past of a German family and a German city and was inspired by many writers of the past; yet it breathed a new spirit and soon became part of world literature, which no German novel had done since the time of Goethe.

The locale of *Buddenbrooks* is the German Baltic city of Lübeck, Mann's birthplace. The city's name is never mentioned, but some of its streets, buildings, and neighboring towns, such as Travemünde, are. A damp wind blows through many scenes, and a gray light predominates.

The story of the four generations of Buddenbrooks begins in 1835 with a joyful, anticipatory, family reunion and ends in 1877 with a sad reunion that is more like a family dissolution. Johann Buddenbrook, Senior, head of a prosperous grain firm founded in 1768, is an old, but lively gentleman imbued with the ideals and tastes of the Enlightenment. He has just acquired a big and stately house in the Mengstraße. Gotthold, Johann Buddenbrook's son by his first wife, is the outcast of the family: he married beneath his social station and opened up a store. Johann Buddenbrook, Jr., his other son, is married to a beautiful and elegant woman, the former Elisabeth Kröger. Soon after his father's death, he has his oldest son, the gifted Thomas, join the firm. His other son, Christian, develops into a hypochondriac playboy. His older daughter, Tony, is pretty and lively, and his younger daughter, Clara, is serious and religious. Tony falls in love with a poor young law student, but, out of a sense of duty and under paternal pressure, she marries Bendix Grünlich, a businessman from Hamburg, for whom she does not care at all. A year later, she has a baby, Erika; but Grünlich, who has been in financial straits, goes bankrupt, and Tony's marriage ends in divorce.

After the death of his father in 1855, Thomas becomes the head of the old firm. He marries the beautiful Gerda, daughter of a rich merchant; Clara marries the Reverend Tiburtius from Riga; and Tony marries Permaneder, a Bavarian hop merchant. Tony's second marriage also ends in divorce. Thomas' election to the Senate is a great triumph, but he is disappointed in his son Hanno, who lacks good health and aggressiveness. Thomas builds a big and beautiful house, but his business and self-confidence are declining. Erika, Tony's daughter, marries Weinschenk, the director of an insurance company. But shortly afterwards Weinschenk is convicted of fraud, and, after three years in prison, disappears from sight. Thomas' mother dies, and the old Buddenbrook house is sold to Thomas' successful competitor, the energetic and urbane Hagenström, a relative newcomer.

Suffering from an infected tooth, Thomas collapses in the middle of the street and dies without regaining consciousness. The firm is liquidated and the new house sold. Hanno, who loves music but hates school—and life in general—dies of typhoid fever, and his mother leaves town.

Mann started to work on *Buddenbrooks* in Italy, where he spent about two years with his brother Heinrich, avoiding any contact with German tourists and residents. According to his own statement, he was encouraged to write this family novel, which also is the novel of *his* family, by the example of the brothers Goncourt and their novel *Renée Mauperin*. For a short time he even thought of collaborating with his brother following the example of the Goncourt brothers. The subtitle of the novel, not given in the standard English translation, reads "Decay of a Family." This suggests French Naturalism and Zola's series of novels on heredity in the Rougon Macquart family. But Mann did not know Zola then and was not concerned with heredity.

[14]

In addition to the Goncourts, he was insipred by Dickens, by Alexander Kielland and Jonas Lie, two minor Norwegian authors of family novels, by Turgenev and Tolstoy, and by the German novelists Theodor Fontane and Fritz Reuter. Yet, Mann's stupendous reading and his many "sources" notwithstanding, *Buddenbrooks* is all his own.

The novel enjoyed almost instantaneous success and in Germany has remained Mann's best-selling novel. And yet it has none of the features of an ordinary best seller. There is no exciting plot, no gripping love story, no popular doctrine. There are no purple passages and no fascinating adventures; just everyday episodes occurring in an upper-middle-class family: weddings and divorces, baptisms and deaths, Christmas parties and outings, holidays at the sea and days at school, new houses and old memories, financial successes and failures, cranks and personalities. But the everyday world is observed by a sharp eye, drawn by a master craftsman, and imbued with atmosphere, sympathy, humor, satire, music, and philosophy.

With some justification, Thomas Mann used to call *Buddenbrooks* the only great naturalist novel in German.[1] His painstaking documentation was indeed that of a naturalist author gathering his data in a scientific way. In notebooks he collected anecdotes about certain people of his native Lübeck, their character traits and typical sayings. He asked his mother to send him the recipe of a festive dish; he prevailed upon a cousin of his father to furnish information about the political and economic life of Lübeck. His sister Julia had to draw up a twenty-eight page report about her aunt, who was to become the Tony Buddenbrook of the novel. There is a key to the "true" identity of almost every figure of the novel.

Mann's realism is often displayed in lengthy descriptions. In the German original, he devotes fourteen lines to the head of a minor figure, the Reverend Tiburtius, seven lines to Thomas' hair, fifteen lines to his hands, twenty-four lines to Permaneder's face, twelve to Hanno's eyes, and seven to the way Hermann Hagenström breathes. There are numerous detailed descriptions of houses and clothes. Some of them have been justly praised for their vividness and brilliance; for example, that of a windy day in the city: "The pavements were wet and dirty; the gray

[15]

gables dipped. But above all stretched the sky, a cloudless tender blue, while millions of atoms of light seemed to dance like crystals in the air" (II, 274).

Mann's realism is also apparent in the occasional use of dialects, the *Plattdeutsch* of Lübeck and the Bavarian of Munich, in the exact time structure, with the many dates given for events in the novel, and in the many precise references to financial assets. Naturalistic preoccupation with the ugly features of human existence can be seen especially in the long description of the painful tooth extraction that precedes Thomas Buddenbrook's death, in the famous six pages devoted to the discussion of typhoid fever, and in the five pages concerned with the agony of Thomas' mother.

But the novel clearly transgresses the boundaries, traditions, and objectives of realistic fiction. It does not pretend to be a social document or to depict social, economic, and political changes for their own sake. That the Hagenströms supplant the Buddenbrooks does not, as has been asserted, signify that a new breed of unscrupulous bourgeois has replaced the old-time patricians. The revolution of 1848 appears like a farce, easily put down by a few well chosen words. The wars of 1866 and 1871 hardly stir any ripples.

Objectivity and ironic detachment are sometimes lost in a romantic feeling for nature and an almost mystical rapture. This is true of Thomas', Hanno's, and, occasionally, even of Tony's feelings for the sea, which make them forget time and life. It is also true of Thomas Buddenbrook's ecstatic vision of the hereafter in which he will live again in many young and strong men, and of Hanno's self-expressive and self-destructive improvisations on the piano.

The description of Hanno's day in school hardly shows realistic detachment, but is a savage satire directed against the stupidity, ineptitude, and rigidity of public education, a caricature in the vein of the magazine *Simplicissimus*, with which Mann was connected for some time before publishing his novel.

Above all, in spite of its biological and sociological trappings, the "decay of the family," one of the central themes of the novel, if not *the* central one, is hardly in tune with naturalistic preoccupations with heredity and environment. It recalls Schopenhauer's duality of will and intellect, is related to Nietzsche's and

Paul Bourget's fascination with modern "decadence," and is the first major expression of Mann's personal and long-lasting feeling that there is a basic contrast between life and intellect, health and sensitivity, normality and art, vitality and beauty. The less vigorous and healthy the Buddenbrooks are, the more religious, intellectual, or artistic they are.

Old Johann Buddenbrook, a strong, aggressive, uncomplicated, successful businessman, is full of life. Life does not seem to have any problems or any depth for him. He dies at the age of seventy-seven. His son, though still a successful businessman, is often dominated by an extreme religious sensitivity, which the reader is supposed to view as an indication of decline. He is the first Buddenbrook to cherish "other than the normal, every-day sentiments proper to good citizens" (I, 260). He dies at fifty-five; the firm's assets have decreased. His daughter Clara dies of tuberculosis at a young age; she "never really cared to live and always longed for heaven" (II, 37). Johann's son Thomas is interested in literature, music, and philosophy, but he is not at home in the "hard practicality of life" (II, 81). He ages prematurely, does not see any purpose or real success in his life, "hates life," and dies at forty-nine. The firm, whose assets have diminished again, has to be dissolved. Thomas' son Hanno is an enthusiastic and talented pianist, but a weak and lonely person. He is "afraid of life" and "disgusted with life." The smell of death is "strangely familiar" to him (II, 284). He is never "disturbed by breakings-up, closings, endings, disintegration" (II, 302). When he dies of typhoid fever at the age of sixteen, it is because he wants to die. Thomas' and Hanno's disgust with life in general, however, has to be seen less as a decadent trait than as young Thomas Mann's own view of life, which he imposed on two of the characters he loved best.

In spite of Thomas Mann's preoccupation with sickness and death, the characters of his novel, including those that are fascinated by death, are brimful of life. They originate in real life and vigorously evoke it. And in spite of the fact that Thomas Mann's and Schopenhauer's pessimism and the end-of-the-century melancholy permeate the book, it reflects a delightful humor and a delight in humor.

With a few masterful strokes, even such minor figures as the grandiloquent broker Gosch and the tiny teacher Sesemi Weichbrodt are sharply and unforgettably delineated. Only Gerda Buddenbrook, Thomas' beautiful, elegant, and musical wife, remains somewhat vague and sketchy; but she is meant to be elusive. To the modern reader, Thomas Buddenbrook is especially interesting, since he eventually shows what is now usually called alienation: an empty and exhausting role-playing. His activity is "something entirely different from his forefathers' natural and permanent fondness for work. It is something artificial, a depressant like the pungent little Russian cigarettes which he is perpetually smoking" (II, 217). His whole existence "is no different from that of an actor. In the absence of any truly ardent interest, his inward impoverishment oppresses him almost without any relief with a constant, dull chagrin; while he stubbornly clings to the determination to be worthily representative" (II, 219). In his "chilled and artificial life," when he falls short of his ambitions as a businessman, as a husband, and as a father, he feels "frightfully lonely" (II, 253).

What raises Thomas Buddenbrook above the crowd of lonely, frustrated, and aging business leaders are, among other things, his cultural interests and, above all, his inner conflict. It is Thomas Mann's own conflict within himself between the bourgeois and the artist, or, as Thomas Buddenbrook puts it, between the hard and practical man and the tender dreamer—a conflict which he calls untenable, unnatural, and exhausting (II, 82). His brother Christian's nonbourgeois way of life was, as he admitted himself, a real temptation for him. He had to struggle against his inclination toward irresponsible loafing and constant introspection in order to gain what he considers the most important thing: control and equilibrium (I, 265). In his early career, he thinks of achieving a gratifying synthesis of the two conflicting forces. His work for his parental firm was largely based on his "idealism," "enthusiasm," "imagination," and, of all things, "a sense of poetry" (I, 274 f.). But later this optimistic outlook is forgotten. His literary taste does not provide any comfort, except for the short and exceptional interest in Schopenhauer; and his feeling for the simple majesty of the sea does not add enjoyment to his life but only makes him temporarily forget its worries and dreariness.

While failure marks only the end of Thomas' life, and only his death is characterized by a lack of dignity, Christian is undignified and a failure throughout his life. This hypochondriac buffoon, amateur entertainer, early devotee of the theater, who constantly complains about his "short nerves" or his difficulties in swallowing, or his suicidal urges, who is unable to work, marries a prostitute, and ends in an insane asylum, is one of Thomas Mann's early caricatures of the artist. On the other hand, little Hanno, who is alienated from most people and unfit for life, who emanates coldness and takes immense and exhausting delight in music, shows the tragic condition of the artist, his loneliness, human coldness, and remoteness from practical, ordinary life.

Tony Buddenbrook, the pretty, but not very intelligent sister of the two antagonistic brothers, is one of Mann's most lovable and humorous creations. Unshaken, though deeply moved by her own and her family's failures, she remains a child throughout, often acting, talking, and crying like a child, but always concerned with the "dignity" of her family. She is the only one who is present on the first and the last page of the long novel. On the first page, she recites, without any understanding or feeling, from the Catechism, while on the last page, she sadly reflects on the many beliefs destroyed by life, a fact which is also a symptom of the unity, irony, and "decay" of the novel.

The vividness and significance of the characters are matched by a superb style. This stylistic richness is much more noteworthy than the intentional repetitions of words and sentences, which have drawn most of the attention directed toward the novel. They are not new in narrative literature. Homer, Tolstoy, Dickens, and the Germans Otto Ludwig, Storm, and Fontane, among others, used them before Mann. They are often called *leitmotifs*. Yet, even though Mann was an early admirer of Wagner, and Wagner's music is played in *Buddenbrooks*, the recurrence of sayings and descriptions hardly possesses a Wagnerian character. Repetitions of sentences in novels, as in radio and television serials, somehow satisfy the desire for familiarity and duration, a desire sharpened in the reader of a novel that depicts constant change and disintegration. Further, the use of the same words in new situations may add a note of poignancy or irony. Above all, the repetitions firmly delineate a person, a street, or a house, and gratify the reader's wish for identification. Sometimes, it must be admitted, a so-called *leitmotif* seems annoyingly mechanical and superfluous. One may wonder, for instance, why one has to be reminded so often of Gerda Buddenbrook's paleness, her red hair, and the blue shadows around her eyes.

The leitmotifs also lend an added measure of unity to the long novel. *Buddenbrooks,* although consisting of two volumes, eleven parts, and ninety-seven chapters, is not a rambling novel with many digressions. Continuity, direction, and firm structure are of its essence. When S. Fischer, a famous publisher, told the young author to shorten his manuscript, Thomas Mann refused. This is indicative of his self-confidence; but the novel actually has no flabby or unessential pages. It has always been a characteristic of Mann's narrative art that facts, events, and persons which at first seem insignificant or trivial, later appear in contrast with, or parallel to, other facts, events, and persons, or reappear in new connections or with variations, thereby acquiring emotional depth or a symbolic dimension.

Another reason why it would have been difficult for the author to make excisions is that the episodes and chapters are often arranged in an antithetical fashion, which gives the events, and life in general, an ironical twist. The chapter containing the mordant satire on Prussian school life ends in Hanno's ecstatic playing at the piano, and is followed by the seemingly cold and scientific chapter on the course of typhoid fever. Toward the end of the centenary celebration of the Buddenbrook firm, in which the whole town participates, the lonely Thomas Buddenbrook receives very depressing financial news. That chapter ends with the poor playing of trivial music, but is followed by a chapter where good musicians play Bach and Wagner. The celebration of Christmas, a greatly moving affair in the Buddenbrook family, is followed by the chapter in which Weinschenk is sentenced to prison, which comes as a heavy blow to the family. The collapse of Tony's second marriage at the end of Part VI is followed by Hanno's baptism at the beginning of Part VII. The paragraph that announces the thirty-seven year old Thomas Buddenbrook's increasing loss of vitality succeeds the chapter in which he is elected Senator, defeating his arch rival Hagenström—a glorious moment in the history of the family.

Originally *Buddenbrooks* was to be about 250 pages long, and was to be mainly concerned with Hanno. But, as in the case of the *Magic Mountain,* later, Mann's thoroughness and ability to manipulate and organize many different facts and thoughts expanded the story considerably. It finally was eleven hundred pages long and covered four generations. Still, the second part begins with Hanno's baptism and ends with his death.

This long family novel, a genuinely German book, has been translated into more than twenty languages. Its mixture of humor and pessimism, realistic observation and romantic emotions, irony and nostalgia, has endeared itself to millions of readers. The "decay of a family" became the firm foundation of Mann's reputation, and it is for *Buddenbrooks* that in 1929 he was awarded the Nobel prize.

CHAPTER 2

The Prince and the Millionaire's Daughter

ROYAL HIGHNESS (1909) surprised and disappointed the reading public. The famous author of the great realistic and pessimistic novel of a bourgeois family, *Buddenbrooks*, had written an apparently light and light-hearted novel about an imaginary court. Somehow, the "decay of a family" seemed so much more important than the decay of a small country. But the novel is not primarily a satirical description of twentieth-century court life, even though Mann, who had done a great deal of "research," includes numerous details of etiquette, titles, and ceremonies.

The novel is, first of all, an allegory of artistic existence. The contrast between life and art, which fascinated and plagued Mann for many years, is shown in the life of Klaus Heinrich, and the synthesis of art and life in his marriage with a commoner. Klaus Heinrich, a "marked man" and a "stranger" (75), symbolizes the artist, as some marked men in Mann's early novellas did. Secondly, the novel concerns itself with the difficulties of extraordinary existence in general, and thirdly, it is an autobiography. It is as much about Mann's courtship as about Albrecht's court.

Mann himself called *Royal Highness* a comedy in the form of a novel, although it has some rather serious, if not tragic, implications and motives. He also called it a rational and didactic fairy-tale. There are numerous realistic and detailed observations of faces, places, and economic conditions, but many elements are treated in the manner of a fairy tale. The prince is redeemed through the love of a beauty. The prophecy of a gypsy woman comes true. No year is given, the country and its capital are not named.

The action of the novel is rather slight. The sickly Albrecht II, Grand Duke of a small German state, asks his brother Klaus Heinrich to assume the duties of official representation in his stead. Klaus Heinrich, who is now addressed as "Royal Highness," leads an empty and unhappy life of make-believe, until he falls in love with Imma Spoelmann, the beautiful daughter of an American multimillionaire who, for reasons of health, has settled in the capital of the Grand Duchy. Imma first distrusts him, because he has done everything for the sake of appearance only, but he convinces her by taking real interest in the community and its grave economic problems. The marriage makes everybody happy, since it saves the economy of the country. The life of the couple will be one of "highness and love—an austere happiness."

The novel, four hundred and seventy pages in the original, consists of a "prelude" and nine chapters with short titles. In the manner of the "preface" to *The Magic Mountain*, the "prelude" to *Joseph*, and the first chapter of *Doctor Faustus*, the short "prelude," which is written in the present tense and describes an everyday scene in the street (Klaus Heinrich meeting a general), announces a major theme: the loneliness and unreality of the "lofty" existence. The novel proper begins with a festive occasion, Klaus Heinrich's birth, and ends with another festive occasion, his wedding. The seventh section of a work by Mann often has great significance. The seventh chapter of *Royal Highness* is by far the largest, covering almost one third of the book. It is called "Imma" in tribute to Katja Mann, the original Imma.

The novel is based on the parallelism between the existence of an artist and that of a prince. There is a reference to the idea, expressed by Schiller in his *Maid of Orleans*, that both the poet and the king dwell on the heights of mankind. Mann has always seen himself as a sort of prince, as he wrote to Katja in September 1904. He once called Hanno Buddenbrook "a prince of decadence," and the education of Adrian Leverkühn, who is another of Mann's self-portraits, is called "princely."

This princely feeling may originally have come from the consciousness of being "carved of the finest wood," as Mann's Felix Krull says about himself; but the analogy between the artist and the prince in *Royal Highness* has other sources. In the years before writing the work, Mann felt that he was leading a cold and impoverished, a merely symbolic or representative existence, resembling that of a prince. No doubt, a recognized artist is expected to "represent" an ideal, a movement, a nation, or greatness in general. In addition, all artists "represent" ideas, feelings, and observations. But few of them would call their lives merely representative and liken them to those of princes. If the artist's life is representative, "symbolic," or "formal," it is because he creates symbols and invents forms. If the prince's life is symbolic or formal, it is so because he is a symbol and lives according to traditional forms.

To young Mann, "formal" meant unreal and unsubstantial. Klaus Heinrich is not "really" a student; he does not study and is not expected to. He is not really an officer; he only wears the uniform. He does not really ask questions during an audience, since he is not really interested in the answers. He expresses opinions, but he really has none (284). There is a connection with the existence of a swindler like Felix Krull, who is not "really" what people think he is. The mere formality of Klaus Heinrich's existence can also alienate people. Like Hanno, Krull, Tonio Kröger, and Adrian Leverkühn, he emanates coldness (157, 284).

Klaus Heinrich's formal existence is a service to the community. It is his duty to edify the people (281). The people need and adore him because, like the artist, he represents what is best in them, their ideals and dreams. He does not control their wishes and aspirations, but expresses these and makes them clear (133). The people are grateful to him because in him they recognize themselves. For the same reason they heartily applaud Mizzi Meyer, a singer who is neither handsome nor talented, but in whom they see their own glorification (159). There is an element of humiliation in this service to the people, and the truly aristocratic Albrecht refuses to express or represent anybody but himself (133).

Significantly, after finishing *Royal Highness,* the allegory of esthetic life, Mann began *Felix Krull,* the parody of artistic existence. Klaus Heinrich's presence transfigures the drabness of everyday life into "poetry"—the connection with the artist is made obvious—, enthusiasm and holiday spirit. The unreality of his activity lends a strange but inspiring veneer of falseness to the reality of the crowds (146-147). Klaus Heinrich knows that the people "sadly need to be elevated above the workday and its reality" (338). He anticipates Felix Krull, who is convinced of the social necessity of illusion.

Although it is formal and insubstantial, Klaus Heinrich's life is difficult, dangerous, and stern (40). It is also lonely and ascetic. He has to suppress human weaknesses, human warmth, and the longing for friends and happiness. When Klaus Heinrich mixes with the crowd at a ball, when he feels and acts like the rest, and thinks that he is "with them," his escapade ends in a humiliating disaster. It is a strenuous and tiring life, too (150). It exhausts him as it did his father and Thomas Buddenbrook, who also lead such a formal life. Similarly, the poets Tonio Kröger and Axel Martini age before their time.

The parallel between artist and prince, the unreality, discipline, and asceticism of their existence, is particularly apparent in the humorous episode concerning Axel Martini, a poet who has won a literary prize for an enthusiastic ode to the joy of life, but whose own life is devoid of all joys and regulated by cautious hygienic considerations. Martini does not drink, does not have any erotic adventures, and must go to bed at ten. "Renunciation is our pact with the Muses," he tells Klaus Heinrich. Life to him is a forbidden garden. To represent life takes all his time and all his effort. He is not allowed to really live, to be happy, or even worried. Like Klaus Heinrich he has had but few experiences. Like Tonio Kröger, he could not write if he actually experienced what he wrote about. Like Tonio Kröger again, he envies, admires, and despises a friend who can enjoy life (166). Although Klaus Heinrich senses the analogy between himself and the poet, he finds him somewhat repulsive (167), but he too is occasionally repellent and meets with hostility and contempt (156). No wonder young Klaus Heinrich is horrified and feels sorry for himself when he first senses the implications of his "exalted calling" (52). The parallel between prince and artist in *Royal Highness* is strengthened by the motive of the physical handicap. Martini's constitution is rather weak; he does not look healthy, and Klaus Heinrich has the handicap of his crippled left arm.

Dr. Überbein, Klaus Heinrich's mentor, is the theoretician of formal existence. He warns his pupil that he is not an individual, but a conception, an ideal, that his extraordinary life must be lonely and disciplined, and even that to represent is something more and higher than simply to be (75, 77). His own life is also ascetic. It is solely devoted to professional achievement and advancement. That he renounces or despises the common joys of life, makes him lonely and extraordinary. Like Klaus Heinrich, he has to overcome a handicap which he acquired at his birth—his illegitimacy. Significantly, when Klaus Heinrich is about to marry a commoner in order to achieve happiness, Überbein commits suicide.

Überbein's friend, Dr. Sammet, a physician who was consulted at Klaus Heinrich's birth and subsequently had a distinguished career, is another person who is driven to extraordinary exertions by the "exceptional obligation" resulting from his extraordinary position. He also has to overcome a handicap acquired from his birth: his being a Jew (20-21).

Like Klaus Heinrich's, Überbein's life is identical with his social function; but in his case the social role is identical with his profession. He is a very dedicated and successful teacher, but Mann repudiates his way of life, or rather his proud rejection of normal, everyday existence. The very name of this over-ambitious, anti-humanistic teacher is probably a satirical reference to Nietzsche's "Übermensch" (superman), an idea which Mann, though a disciple of Nietzsche, never accepted.

Like Klaus Heinrich, Überbein, and Dr. Sammet, Mr. Spoelmann and his daughter Imma were born into their extraordinary existence (173, 219). One petitioner actually calls Spoelmann "Royal Highness" (249). Spoelmann, who is neither a prince nor an artist, and Imma actually "understand the duty of representation which an extraordinary existence imposes" (184, 237). Abnormality, a symptom of extraordinary existence, is shown in the novel particularly by Imma's deranged lady companion, the countess Löwenjoul, and by the equally aristocratic and deranged collie Perceval.

The rosebush, which has been growing for many years in a courtyard of the Old Castle, is a symbol of extraordinary existence, abnormality, decadence, and formal, i.e. "soulless" life. "It seems as if it had no soul," Imma says (260). Its flowers are beautiful but have a scent of decay. There is a popular belief that they will start giving forth a natural and lovely odor on a day of general rejoicing (35). The bush is given by Albrecht to his brother as a wedding gift; it is transplanted into a garden where there are no "moulding walls," but sunshine and air. This specifically symbolizes decadence in a fine, old family and the conquest of decadence through love and a new active life. Although, significantly enough, the last chapter is called "The Rosebush," only one paragraph of that chapter is devoted to it (332). Since the novel ends with the May wedding, the reader does not find out whether the roses actually acquire a sweet scent.

The autobiographical nature of the novel is evident. Like Mann, Klaus Heinrich is born in early June. His older brother has the features of Mann's older brother Heinrich. Imma Spoelmann has many traits of Mann's wife Katja: she is beautiful, bright, has dark eyes, black hair, a "pearl white" face, and studies mathematics. When Mann wrote the novel, he reread the letters he had written to his fiancée in 1904. Like Klaus Heinrich, Mann watched Katja through an opera glass before he met her. Like Imma, Katja showed Mann her mathematics books. Mann and Katja used to go bicycling together, as Klaus Heinrich and Imma do with horseback riding. Once, when Mann had a sore throat, Katja's father got up from his couch and gave him a creased piece of oil silk, as Imma's father does in the same situation (279). The name Klaus Heinrich is that of Mann's oldest son, born in 1906: Klaus Heinrich Thomas Mann. Klaus was the first name of Katja's twin brother, and Heinrich that of Mann's older brother. Finally, the impossible and aristocratic collie Perceval is drawn after Mann's own collie Motz.

The style is marked by numerous leitmotifs. Most of them refer to physical characteristics, such as the high and wide cheekbones of the common people (and of Klaus Heinrich), Imma's black hair, white face, and pursed lips, or to the "difficult," "extraordinary," "lofty," and "austere" life of "decorum."

At its publication, *Royal Highness* was dwarfed by *Buddenbrooks;* it is even more dwarfed today by *The Magic Mountain* and *Joseph.* It suffers somewhat from its dubious theory of "formal" life and from a certain paleness and tameness; there is not a single villain in it. But it is an appealing success story of a modest and likeable young man.

CHAPTER 3

Education in a Sanitarium

IN 1912, Mann visited his wife at a sanitarium for tuberculosis patients in Davos. He caught a bad cold and was advised by the physicians to stay for at least half a year; but he left at the end of three weeks. His observations and experiences in the sanitarium prompted him to write a humorous short story about the "magic mountain." He started work in 1913, but during the war years all his creative writing stopped, for he was mostly and deeply concerned with Germany's cultural position in the modern world. His ideas were published toward the end of the war in a collection of essays, *Reflections of a Non-Political Man*, but many found their way, in a modified or fictionalized form, into *The Magic Mountain*, which finally appeared in 1924 as a weighty novel of two volumes. It became an immediate international success, although it was far from being a conventional novel.

Hans Castorp, a young engineer from Hamburg, visits his cousin Joachim in the "Berghof," a luxury sanitarium in Davos. He plans to relax there for three weeks, but the new atmosphere changes his outlook; he falls in love with Clavdia Chauchat, a Russian lady, catches a bad cold, a "moist spot" is discovered in his lungs, and he stays seven years in the sanitarium, where he is completely alienated from the normal world. He expands his horizon, thanks to his interest in disease, his readings, and his discussions with the rationalist Settembrini and the irrationalist Jesuit Naphta. His cousin dies. Clavdia, who had left the sanitarium, returns in the company of Peeperkorn, a wealthy plantation owner. After Peeperkorn's suicide she leaves again. The outbreak of World War I ends the general stupor and irritation in the *Berghof* and the world at large. Castorp rushes home and is last seen on the battlefield.

The Magic Mountain belongs to several different literary genres. As the author indicates in his preface, Hans Castorp's story has something of the fairy tale or the legend about it. The title itself, *Der Zauberberg*, has been used as another name for the Brocken mountain, scene of the Walpurgis Night gathering of witches, according to German folklore. The last section of the first volume is actually called "Walpurgis Night," although it takes place on the night of mardi gras rather than on April 30. There is also an echo of the legendary *Hörselberg*, where the minnesinger Tannhäuser spent some time with Venus. The *Hörselberg* is particularly suggested by the "grotto of the mountain of sin" ("state of sin" in the standard translation, 894). Mann mentions the connection between the novel and the *Hörselberg* in the sketch of his life written in 1930.

Hans Castorp, with his seven years' service ("Kurdienst"), is perhaps also a counterpart to another Hans, "Hans im Glück" ("Hans in Luck"), the protagonist of the Grimm fairy tale, who served his master for seven years. There is, toward the end, an allusion to another legend, the "Seven Sleepers of Ephesus" (687, lost in the translation on p. 894). The number seven, which is in evidence in many legends and fairy tales, is a sort of fundamental number in the *Magic Mountain.*

The number of Clavdia's door is 7, that of Castorp's is 34 (3 + 4 = 7). Castorp is orphaned at seven and he makes the fateful decision to leave for Davos "in the last days of July" (the seventh month) of 1907. Joachim decides to return to the *Berghof* at the end of July and Castorp stays there for seven years (In his Princeton lecture on the *Magic Mountain,* Mann calls them the seven fairy-tale years). He spends a night, the only night, with Clavdia after seven months at the *Berghof.* The thermometer has to be kept in the mouth for seven minutes. There are seven tables in the dining room; and a group of seven people takes the excursion to the waterfall. Toward the end of his stay in the *Berghof,* Castorp sits at a table with six others; and at seven p.m. he has his strange and perhaps symbolic experience of seeing broad day and a moonlit landscape at the same time (197-198; the hour is lost in the translation). At one point before his departure for the plains, Joachim has been in the sanitarium seven times seventy days (535); he dies at seven p.m. At the end, the volunteers march for seven hours.

The novel has seven chapters; the first volume ends after seven months; and the crucial section "Snow" is the seventh section of chapter VI.

The novel offers an abundance of names with seven letters: Clavdia, Castorp, Joachim, Ziemßen, Marusja, Behrens, Lukaček, Berghof; Mynheer (Peeperkorn) probably belongs here, too. In Settembrini's name, the Italian word for seven is audible. Settembrini is also between thirty and forty years old (73), two numbers that add up to seventy. And his opponent Naphta has "about the same age" (471).

This preference for the number seven is, however, due not only to the influence of fairy tales and legends. Mann had an almost superstitious belief in the significance of certain numbers. For years he was sure that he would die at the age of seventy. The narrator of *The Magic Mountain* says of the number seven that it is "a good, handy figure in its way, picturesque, with a savor of the mythical; one might even say that it is more filling to the spirit than a dull academic half dozen" (887).

While the *Magic Mountain* is meant to be a twentieth-century fairy tale or legend, it also follows the tradition, though not quite the spirit, of the German *Bildungsroman* (also called *Erziehungsroman* or *Entwicklungsroman*), the novel of education or development, whose most noteworthy example is Goethe's *Wilhelm Meister*. For the engineer Hans Castorp, the "magic mountain" is a sort of postgraduate school, lasting seven years, with lab sessions, readings, lectures, and discussions. The two "courses" which he has to take are the experiences of disease and death. His "electives" comprise philosophy, theology, foreign languages (French), botany, astronomy, anatomy, physical education (skiing), physiology, histology, physics, mathematics, chemistry, pathology, pharmacology, the fine arts (painting), radiology, parapsychology, psychoanalysis, embryology, bacteriology, meteorology, music, and political science. There is a curious absence of literature proper. Castorp does not read or discuss any novels or poems, and there is hardly any allusion to writers; Leopardi and Dante being some of the exceptions.

Because his education is "hermetic" (a word that suggests seclusion from fresh air, but also shrewdness, magic, and myth) or "alchemic," Castorp not only makes very rapid progress, but also utilizes the many different sciences and observations to become an integral part of his feeling and thinking,[1] not just, as so often happens in ordinary education, deadwood to be quickly discarded and forgotten. This also has aesthetic implications. The paragraphs or pages on the lymph, or the nature of life, or on X-rays, for instance, do not remain extraneous matter, but form an integral part of the novel. They may even produce humorous or ironical effects: Castorp, for instance, supports his frenzied declaration of love to Clavdia with anatomical terminology; and he recalls the chemistry of tears when he cries at his cousin's death (677).

It has been justly observed that in a typical novel of education the hero, after going through many experiences, matures into a well-adjusted member of society, while in *The Magic Mountain* Castorp starts out as what many would consider a well-adjusted or typical member of society, bent on a useful occupation; but after being subjected to the "magic" pedagogy, he seems forever separated from normal life, to which he does not wish to return. Incidentally, Castorp's educational experience is sometimes referred to not as that of a student who learns from his teachers or "mentors," but as that of a man who takes a trip for the sake of his education ("Bildungsreisender," partly lost on 725).

The Magic Mountain is not only a fairy tale in modern dress and a novel of education, but it has also much in common with the realistic novel of the nineteenth and twentieth centuries, which objectively depicts contemporary society. The rather specialized world of the sanitarium must indeed be viewed as a reflection of and on society in general. *The Magic Mountain* lacks, however, the narrative sweep, the exciting plot, the variety of figures of the novels of a Balzac or Tolstoy, for instance, or even of *Buddenbrooks*. It is also much more concerned with the well-to-do than with the poor and the manual workers, and more with the middle-aged than with children and the very old.

The narrator of the novel implies that his story is a *Zeitroman*, which usally means a novel about contemporary life and contemporary problems,[2] but he also declares that the word *Zeitroman* could have another meaning: a novel about the nature of time. *The Magic Mountain* obviously is a *Zeitroman* in both senses, as Mann affirms in his lecture on the novel, delivered before students at Princeton in 1939.

The novel's realism is conspicuous. Davos and its environment are described accurately with many proper names. The careful rendering of life in the sanitarium, which does not omit the repulsive and the trivial, has made many readers believe that Mann's main intention was to satirize the medical profession. Numerous persons are vividly portrayed in their external appearance, clothing, speech, and mannerisms; Dr. Behrens, the chief physician, being an outstanding example. Some descriptions may seem to be excessively long, such as the one of the gramophone, which covers more than a page. Whether, however, the long and sharp verbal duels between Settembrini and Naphta, Castorp's great dream during his ski excursion, and Joachim's ghost are still within the limits of a realistic novel is open to debate.

The Magic Mountain can also be labeled a symbolic novel, since its deeper meaning can only be gauged if Castorp, Naphta, Peeperkorn, or the *Berghof* are also understood as symbols. The narrator's remarks on the symbolic importance of the "Lindenbaum" clearly points in this direction (819).

Finally, *The Magic Mountain* is a novel of ideas, perhaps the "supreme German novel of ideas."[3] However, it does not develop or present a definite ideology. It is not an illustration of a philosophical, sociological, or political system, but rather delights and excels in showing the clash and interplay of many ideas.

The *Magic Mountain* was originally planned as a humorous counterpart to the tragic "Death in Venice." The comic effects stem from the conflict between macabre adventure and bourgeois respectability, from odd figures, such as the ignorant Mrs. Stöhr, who refers to Beethoven's "Erotica," from puns and jokes, such as those made by Dr. Behrens, and, on a higher level, from the narrator's attitude to his work and to his readers.

In the novella and in the novel, we encounter a fascination with death and the triumph of disorder over a disciplined life. In both there is also the feeling of love toward a fourteen-year-old boy with a Slavic name, the general atmosphere of sickness, the resort life (for life at the *Berghof* is once called that of a bathing resort, "resortish scene," 144), and an important symbolic dream with classical Greek elements. For reasons of self-preservation, both Aschenbach and Castorp should not have stayed in their vacation spot. They both stay because of their irrational love and their love of the irrational. But there are important

differences. While the accomplished master's creativity and
sense of responsibility are destroyed by his experiences in Venice,
the "simple" Castorp widens his educational horizon considerably
and magically grows to become a "man of genius" or, as some
critics put it, an integrated personality, who feels the responsibility to "take stock" of his newly won ideas and insights.

Mann's narrative treatment of time is remarkable. He spends
almost as many pages on Castorp's first three weeks in the sanitarium as on his last five years there. This can be explained
from the point of view of young Castorp, for whom the first
weeks at the *Berghof* are full of new and startling experiences,
while later on, when nothing exciting happens, time flies fast
and unnoticed. But in order to stress the dullness of Castorp's
later years in the sanitarium, the author omits giving any indica-
tions of time from Joachim's death on. Thus it is impossible to
say when Clavdia Chauchat returns. Hans does not even know
how long Joachim has stayed in the sanitarium or how long he
has been away (685), which the reader can tell if he cares to
do some figuring. After his cousin's death, Hans does not even
know how long he himself has stayed in the *Berghof* nor how old
he is. This may be difficult to explain in a predominantly realistic
novel. For even though Castorp has neither watch nor calendar
and reads no newspaper, and even though his interest in time
has been lost, there are numerous factors that could or should
have prevented, remedied, or alleviated this condition. The
weekly bills, which he still pays, are dated. There certainly are
clocks and calendars in the sanitarium. The meals are taken at
fixed hours. There are new patients with a normal interest in
dates. There are celebrations of Christmas, New Year's Eve,
mardi gras, birthdays, and so on.

Castorp's disregard for the passing of time is not accidental.
He has long been receptive to the feeling that time has stopped
its flow. This "hermetic enchantment" with timelessness is even
called "the fundamental adventure of his soul" (890). The reason why little Hans liked to ask his grandfather to show him the
baptismal bowl, which had served so many generations, was his
desire to experience and enjoy the feeling of time as both flowing
and persisting, of recurrence in continuity (30). On his first day
in the *Berghof*, when everybody sits down for lunch, he has the
dreamy impression as if the guests had never left their seats.

He likes this impression and tries to retain it. And years later, at the barber's or when paring his nails, he is often suddenly overpowered by "a mixture of terror and eager joy that make him fairly giddy," incapable of distinguishing between "now" and "then" ("still" and "again"), and prone to mingle these in a timeless eternity (687-688).

Castorp knows that this "indulgence in attacks of mysticism" is "reprehensible," and tries to counteract it, at first. But he finally succumbs to the "dizzying problem of identities" (of still, again, and next; or of yesterday, today, and tomorrow), to his "vicious time-economy and baleful traffic with eternity" (688-691). Mann neither advocates nor greatly exonerates this mysticism. He thinks that there is only one situation where such a "confusion and obliteration of distances in time" is justified, and that only for a few hours during a vacation: the stroll on the beach (689-690). As Mann affirmed a few years before the publication of the *Magic Mountain* in his canine idyll "A Man and His Dog," only the sight and sound of water could ever make him forget time and space. He foisted his experience of timelessness upon some figures of his creation and liking: Hanno, Tonio Kröger, and Castorp. This experience is intensified in Castorp by the "hermetic magic".[4]

In order to stress or explain Castorp's confusion in time, Mann frequently shows the confusion of the seasons in Davos: It snows in August, and the sun can be very strong in winter. Throughout the novel (not just toward the end), he also seems to avoid specific dates, contrary to his usage in *Buddenbrooks*. The narrator's point of view, though ordinarily it purports to be objective, is dominated by Castorp's view point. To be sure, there is Christmas 1907, mardi gras 1908, and an incidental September 26, 1907 (280), but we don't know Castorp's birthday, the day of his arrival at or departure from the *Berghof*, of Joachim's departure, of Peeperkorn's arrival, and so on. We only know that Joachim has been at the *Berghof* for more than five months when Castorp arrives there "in the very first days of August," 1907. Incidentally, in this instance at least, the curious and attentive reader, with the help of a perpetual calendar, can find out the exact date. Since Hans arrived on Tuesday (205), it was August 6. Castorp's first full day at the *Berghof* was August 7, which is in line with Mann's number symbolism.

[34]

The experience of timelessness is not the only trait that Castorp shares with Thomas Mann. Like his creator, he was born into a respected, well-to-do family residing in a North German port, is an indifferent student at school, but an excellent and voracious reader after leaving school, reads "with a pencil," visits a relative in a sanitarium for lung diseases in Davos, is told to stay longer because of sickness, likes music, loves the sea, enjoys playing the gramophone, is fascinated by disease and death, has a good command of French, is "phlegmatic," does not go to church, is conservative in his attire, smokes too much, and feels seasick when he participates in the "occult experiences."

Castorp's spiritual development corresponds vaguely to that of Mann. He is attracted by the ideals of Western Enlightenment—whose major spokesman, Voltaire, was greatly admired by Mann—as well as by irrationality and Romanticism. Like Mann, Castorp fights, or at least dreams, his way through the "love of death" to the love of life.

But Castorp does not equal Thomas Mann. Mann's ideas are often expressed by other figures. In some respects, the "problem child of life" is the very opposite of his author. At any rate, at thirty, Castorp is a lonely man without any accomplishments, inactive, and bogged down in stupid hobbies. Mann, at thirty, was a famous and a happily married writer of fiction. And though Castorp is much more than the simple and dull, though appealing, young man he is made out to be in the beginning, his intellectual stature is far below that of his creator. As in the case of *Wilhelm Meister,* the education of the protagonist of this novel of education constitutes only a fragment or a symbol of the author's education.

Still, Castorp's education is quite remarkable, perhaps even incredible, both as regards the speed and the quality of his achievements. He soon leaves the merely receptive stage, becomes critical of both his teachers, discovers their lack of consistency, formulates ideas of his own, invents paradoxes and wordplays, coins witticisms, and develops a respectable oratory. His education is accelerated and intensified by his other pedagogical influences, which in a way, are related to each other: his disease or the atmosphere of disease, his love of Clavdia, and his feelings for death. One notes that while disease, according to some utterances in the novel (126, 588) and in line with remarks by Novalis, Heine, and Nietzsche, may elevate a person to the rank of genius, Castorp is the only one in the T.B. amusement park who demonstrates this "transsubstantiation." The pedagogical alchemy of sickness, sex, and death does not work on the others, who remain as frivolous, stupid, and uninspiring as before.

But the allegedly simple Castorp has some talents and predispositions for his "hermetic" rise. He has a history of pulmonary disease, of being fascinated by death ("When somebody dies, I feel quite in my element," 141), of enjoying the obliteration of time limits, and of unreasonable love (of Pribislav Hippe). He also is a rascal and cunning, as the narrator, Settembrini, and Settembrini's *bête noire*, Clavdia, repeatedly assert (258, 495, 717, lost on 755). While in the beginning he seems a "regular guy," for whom "a day without tobacco would be flat, stale, and unprofitable" (64), it soon turns out that he has been critical of contemporary society, the cruelty and snobbishness of the bourgeoisie (254); and that contemporary life has had no meaning for him (293). This "hollow silence" which "life about him opposed to all the questions as to the final, absolute, and abstract meaning in all his efforts and activities" (41-42) is one of the reasons why he stays on in the *Berghof* and is eager to learn and experiment (as the "thunderclap" is the reason why he leaves the *Berghof*). That he ever put these "questions," "consciously or unconsciously," shows that he is not just another aspiring young engineer.

Castorp's erotic life seems to be as atypical for a resident of the *Berghof* as is his education. The general atmosphere at the sanitarium, particularly the prevailing idleness, stimulates and facilitates flirtation and more than flirtation, and the combination or even identity of disease and "love" is constantly stressed in the novel. In his first seven months, Castorp only thinks of Clavdia and, after the one night with her, has no sexual experience for the rest of his sojourn at the *Berghof*, although after her return Clavdia once kisses him on his mouth and he kisses her on the forehead. He does not seem to be sexually interested in any other woman.

But although Castorp differs in his love life and his education from the rest, at the end he succumbs to the general stupor, and like everybody else he rushes to the war. If it were not for his one dream of love and kindness, one almost could ask the question: "Hermetic" education, for what?

Mann once explained the great success of *The Magic Mountain* in Germany by the fact that in Castorp the German reader recognized himself. Quite obviously Castorp "stands" for Germany, being in the middle between the West (Settembrini) and the East (Naphta and Clavdia). But while it may be easy for some reader to see in young Hans some "typical" German traits, it might also be easy to notice traits that are not usually thought of in connection with Germans. Castorp's interest in music has been taken as a German trait. Indeed Mann often expressed the thought that in Germany music was playing the great role that literature did in France; therefore, his "Doctor Faustus" is a musician. But Castorp's love of music is purely receptive, comes late in the novel (except for a brief statement, 154); and of his favorite five records three are French and one Italian.

Old nations have changed so often and produced so many different individuals that it is impossible to state with certainty what is characteristic of them. Any such statement is characteristic only of the person who makes it or the one to whom it is addressed. Thus Settembrini's crude remark to Castorp, "Beer, tobacco, and music: Behold the Fatherland!" (145), is perhaps characteristic of an ironical "Western" writer, while Clavdia's "Bourgeois, humanist, and poet—there is the perfect German" (425) is characteristic of the rather independent Russian lady's contempt for the bourgeois. Both remarks can hardly be reconciled with each other or with German reality. When Clavdia states that Germans live for the enrichment of their selves rather than passionately, she may have Castorp in mind, as he himself implies (749). While Settembrini and Clavdia often look at Castorp as a representative of Germany, Castorp himself never boasts of or stresses his typically German traits; and when he rushes to the war, there is no allusion to his patriotic enthusiasm, to German ideals or rights. On the battlefield he is humming the "Lindenbaum," not the "Deutschlandlied."

Settembrini is Castorp's first educator in the *Berghof;* indeed he starts his pedagogical efforts on the very first day. He is also the only one left at Castorp's departure. Hans sometimes thinks of him as a windbag; at one time he is even insolent toward him (798), but he likes him. Settembrini takes personal interest in Hans, which Naphta does not. When he calls Hans "life's problem child," it is because he has become *his* problem child. He is the only one to take leave of Castorp when the latter departs for the war. He embraces and kisses him, even calls him by his first name, which only Joachim did before (and that only once) and uses the *du* form, which only Joachim and, occasionally, Clavdia and Peeperkorn did before.

This "organ grinder" always wears the same slightly worn outfit, perhaps because he always uses the same old slogans. A collaborator of a new encyclopedia, he is the representative of the Enlightenment, whose main arsenal in the eighteenth century was the *Encyclopédie*. He therefore stands and, above all, talks for reason, progress, activity, democracy. He extols literature, enjoys clarity, eloquence, a "plastic" enunciation, and warns against the dangers of paradoxes and music.

Often referred to as a "Literat," he is what Mann once called a "Zivilisationsliterat." Against the German variety of "Zivilisationsliterat," Mann had directed his bitter satire in his *Reflections of a Non-Political Man*. In these somewhat tortured and confused essays, he opposed what he thought were German values to those supposedly typical of the Western European countries: culture to civilization, music to politics, spirit (or art) to literature, soul to society, inner freedom to democracy, and irony to radicalism. Settembrini is the spokesman of the Western traits or ideals, but Mann had mellowed since the War. The German Castorp is not Settembrini's antithesis but his student; he stands cautiously and critically, but not defiantly, in the middle between the West and the East. Settembrini's provocative statement, "Everything is politics," sounded less harsh to Mann's ears in the twenties, since he was himself no longer a "non-political man."

Mann often said that the French, unlike the English, were "dry," i.e., lacked humor. Of Settembrini, whom Castorp finds somewhat "dry" (lost on 117, 128), he once says that he never laughs (307); but in other passages he mentions Settembrini's laughter (306, 656, lost on 866). This contradiction is not disturbing in a novel where a major theme is that life and thought are full of contradictions.

Leo Naphta, Settembrini's sparring partner, once calls antithesis the "moving, the passionate, the dialectic principle of all Spirit" (474). He himself is a living antithesis. Son of an orthodox Jew who was hanged by Christian fanatics, he began his career in the Jesuit order; an admirer of monastic life, he advocates violence, torture, and communism; a Jesuit teacher, he challenges another intellectual to a duel with pistols; a terrorist, he does not want to shoot his opponent in the duel; an ascetic, he likes luxury; a detractor of rationalism, he argues with sharp logic; an advocate of the Church, he commits suicide; a very learned man, he derides science. He is more brilliant but also less appealing than Settembrini. He is a confusing advocate of irrationalism, romanticism, neo-primitivism, ultra-conservatism, and totalitarianism. His historical models include the late Nietzsche and Georges Sorel. His model in life is the Hungarian Communist historian and critic Georg Lukács, for whom Mann once intervened with the Austrian authorities and who wrote an admiring book on Mann. One notices the same vowels in the two first names (Georg, Leo) and the fact that Naphta lives in the apartment of a Lukaček.[5] Curiously enough, Naphta commits suicide while Lukács is still alive twelve years after Mann's death.

Clavdia Chauchat, who precedes Naphta in opposing Settembrini, may be, etymologically speaking, a "hot cat" (French *chaud chat*), but she is not a dumb and flirtatious sex kitten. She does not try very hard to allure Castorp or any other man, grants Castorp one night and leaves the day after, does not renew the intimate relationship after Peeperkorn's death, but leaves again and never writes to him. She is mature, educated, sensitive, and intelligent. Some of her remarks, such as the one that being moral may imply abandoning oneself to sin (430), express Mann's own opinions. Her great respect and deep concern for Peeperkorn, her enrolling Castorp as an ally in the defense of the "man of format," show a human depth uncommon in a mere flirt. Indeed, the adjective "human," which she uses quite often, fits her even better than would "feminine."

To be sure, she has feminine charm, beautiful arms; but, strangely enough, Castorp's feeling for her are a continuation and revival of his love of Pribislav. Her voice, her slanted eyes, and her high cheek bones remind him of the young boy with whom he was infatuated about ten years ago. He sometimes even identifies Clavdia with Pribislav. His French and frenzied hymn after Whitman is mostly not about Clavdia's, not even about the female body, but about the human body in general. Clavdia represents the lure of the feminine less than that of sex, or even that of the strange, the foreign (particularly Russian), the irresponsible, the disorderly, the unreasonable, and the primitive.

The wealthy Peeperkorn, in whose company Clavdia returns to the *Berghof*, represents the "great personality." His greatness seems to consist of an impressive face, large gestures, friendliness and understanding, and an almost religious belief in the simple joys of life: nature, food, and sex. He towers above the crowd of average people, and his mere presence silences or obscures the brilliant discussions of the two pedagogues. But, ironically, this great personality rarely finishes a sentence, often makes no sense whatever, and is introduced at a time when he is already sick and unable to enjoy sex. And this great apostle of vitality commits suicide. Mann was fascinated by the problem of the great personality, perhaps because he felt that he himself lacked it. Peeperkorn reminds one of Dionysos, of Tolstoy, sometimes even of Christ, but his model in life was the great German dramatist Gerhart Hauptmann, whose face, manner of speaking, and generous consumption of alcohol Peeperkorn has inherited. Mann, who greatly admired Hauptmann, felt sometimes uneasy about this parody.

The section "Snow" is the artistic and intellectual climax of *The Magic Mountain*. It contains a brilliant description of a snow storm—one of the pinnacles of realist literature—, the contradictory feelings and thoughts of a person lost in a blizzard, on the verge of succumbing to the temptation of lying down, a "great" dream, and the dream interpretation during the dream itself, which carries the novel's message. "Snow" is not just a recapitulation of the preceding part, as is generally thought, since Castorp goes beyond Settembrini and Naphta (indeed rejects them both as mere talkers), has new ideas, and creates a new ideal, which, to be sure, he forgets as soon as he reaches the safety of the *Berghof*, though he promised that he would remember (626).

In his interpretation, Castorp extols life, love, and man. After months of fascination with sickness and death, he now maintains that "all interest in disease and death is only another expression of interest in life" (624). And while his declaration of love to

Clavdia had culminated in a French ode to "Liebestod," an identification of sickness, love, and death, he now recognizes that
"death and love don't go together," and that "love" is stronger
than death" (626). To be sure, this powerful "love" is kept
vague, but it is certainly different from the "amour" of the Walpurgis Night, which is a synonym of sex. It is opposed to
society's peacetime cruelty (254) as well as to its hate during
the war. It may be related to the "love of humankind" with
which, according to Settembrini, humanism is identical (202).
Castorp now also sees the weakness of dialectical reasoning and,
having already noticed the great confusion in Settembrini's and
Naphta's contradictory arguments before his adventure in the
snow (589), he now declares that "man is the lord of counter-
positions," that man's position is in the middle between the
opposites (625). Castorp's new triad—life, love, man—reappears
later in his conversation with Clavdia: "Love of death leads to
love of life and love of man" (752). Only that "love of death"
seems rather strong compared to the previous "interest in death"
or to the "silent recognition of the blood-sacrifice" which the
"Children of the Sun" have.

Castorp scoffs at the alleged contrasts of death and life, disease
and health, spirit and nature. Mann himself seems to recant here
his own long dialectical thinking and his favorite contrasts. Long
before encountering the beautiful dream landscape where opposites are conquered, Castorp sees a real landscape where they
co-exist. Later, these opposites stand symbolically for two
opposed cultural worlds (tradition and rebellion): One part
of the countryside is still dominated by daylight and the other
part already immersed in moonlight. Castorp's rejection of sharp
delineations and oppositions subsequently leads him to a view
which disregards or denies limits as seen by the ordinary observer. He finds, for instance, the boundary lines between
actuality and fraud fluid (838); he sees no border lines between
stupidity and cleverness (736), or between devotion and egoism
(749). The narrator joins him by drawing no clear-cut distinc-
tions between the "soulful" and the "passionate" in love (755).

The dream interpretation ends in the only sentence in the
whole novel which is in italics: *For the sake of goodness and
love, man shall let death have no sovereignty over his thoughts"*
(626). This does not mean that Castorp's or Mann's fascination

with death has ended. Castorp will still "keep faith with death in his heart," for "death is a great power," which has to be honored. But "faith with death and the dead is evil, is hostile to humankind, as soon as we give it power over thought and action" (626). Death's power over thought and action probably means the psychological, social, and political influence of what man has outgrown, means neo-barbarism, means Naphta. This warning against the dangers of what is no longer timely is sounded more often and more strongly in the *Joseph* tetralogy.

The section "Snow" has ties not only with the end of the first volume, but also with the end of the second volume. The three sections are interconnected. While "Snow" contains the dream of a beautiful Utopia, an ideal landscape, and a creed of love stronger than death, of man being more aristocratic than life, death, and thought, the "dream" at the end of the book shows the landscape of ugly reality, of raging "fever" and death, of man being wretched and expendable. At the end, the author only wonders whether out of this "universal feast of death," this "desperate dance," one day "Love shall mount." While Castorp, in his dream, self-consciously observes the life of the Children of the Sun, we are self-conscious witnesses of the young soldiers' fighting and dying. The strange metaphors of "feast" and "dance" for war and battle probably come from the connection of this last scene with the Walpurgis Night, from which a certain "love" did "mount." Mann does not narrate the consummation of Castorp's love at the end of volume I, nor does he report the end of Castorp's life at the end of volume II.

In "Snow," Castorp rises to become a representative of mankind, and he knows it. His adventure in the snow storm is symbolic of human history. Man has been fighting his way through the hostility or indifference of the elements. His will or urge to live and reach his goal is stronger than the temptation of inertia or the lure of nihilism. Man's ideal, of which, however, he is not always conscious, is an active, happy, civilized society, where kindness and mutual respect prevail, in spite, or because, of the ever present cruelty of human fate and the horror of death. Mann often expounded this new humanism in the years following the *Magic Mountain*. It is because of the humanist character of his Utopia that Castorp's dream landscape is Mediterranean. Mann turned again to this landscape, and for a longer stay, in his next novel, the *Joseph* tetralogy.

CHAPTER 4

Back to the Patriarchs

JOSEPH *and his Brothers* is a tetralogy, an epic in four volumes. The first two were published in Berlin in 1933 and 1934, respectively, the third in Vienna in 1936, the fourth in Stockholm in 1943. Much of the third volume was written in exile in Switzerland, all of the fourth in California. The dates and places point at the turmoil of the times and at the unrest in Mann's existence. Ironically, the "Prelude" mentions the restlessness of the narrator. Like the *Magic Mountain,* the story of Joseph was planned as a novella; but after sixteen years of work it finally emerged as a "narrative of seventy thousand calmly flowing lines," to use Mann's own words (p. V).

Mann was encouraged to write his work by Goethe's remark in *Dichtung und Wahrheit* that the Joseph story in the Bible was "natural," but needed more body. As an adolescent, Goethe himself had written a prose epic about Joseph. In Mann's version, the "natural tale" (535) appears quite sophisticated and possesses not only a new, large and beautiful body but also displays a new and exciting spirit.

It is amazing that much of the vast and vastly comic prose epic was written during a time of tragic upheaval. But the work was Mann's "refuge, comfort, and home," as he declares in the "Foreword" to the one-volume American edition. At a time when anti-Semitism in Germany was at its height, a German author wrote about the ancestors of the Jews. At a time when the dangerous present seemed to demand all of man's attention, Mann wrote about mythology, prehistory, and ancient history. To be sure, he "humanized" myth, turning it against the neo-barbarians who extolled and exploited it as a way of, and pretext for, dehumanization.

The tetralogy transcends the boundaries of the conventional novel. In spite of Mann's wide, scientific readings and the authenticity of many of his descriptions, the tetralogy is not a historical or religious novel; it was not intended to be. Mann relishes the irony of frequent anachronisms and of mixing different mythologies and religions. He is less concerned with the peculiarities of people living in a particular time and country than with man in general. In a sense, the stage of the novel is the universe; the time, eternity. Man's "riddling essence is the alpha and omega of all his questions" (3), and it is "man's nature" which he delights in seeking out in the "underworld" (33) of the past of more than three thousand years ago.

Surprising even to the author himself, quite unusual for him, and in contrast to the cosmic speculations, the sophisticated allusions, the scholarliness, and the ironies, are the naïve tenderness and "paradigmatic" simplicity of certain episodes, of Jacob's meeting Rachel, for instance, of his very long courtship, of Rachel's death, and of the reconciliation of the brothers. He had to cry when he wrote the episode of Rachel's death and whenever he read it again. Ruben's "shame-faced" affection toward his conceited brother and Jacob's paternal love are some of the other heart-warming experiences of the eternally human. The simple grandeur of the recognition scene may be somewhat spoiled by Joseph's urge to stage and "decorate" it as a play, but even this brilliant stage manager cannot help crying.

Although the author also deals with Joseph's ancestors and, to some extent, goes back as far as the creation of the world, the narration proper extends from Joseph's seventeenth to his fifty-seventh year. The narrator, at one point, states that he never planned to go beyond. The "Prelude" to the first volume ("Descent into Hell") stands somewhat apart; it has not even a chapter number. This is also true of the "Prelude in the Upper Circles" which precedes the third volume. Each volume has seven chapters ("Hauptstücke"). The first one, *The Tales of Jacob,* is mainly concerned with Joseph's ancestors, i.e. Abraham, Isaac, and particularly his father Jacob; the second, *Young Joseph,* with his relation to his father and his brothers; the third, *Joseph in Egypt,* with his life at Peteprê's and, particularly, with his dealings with Peteprê's wife, Mut; the fourth, *Joseph the Provider,* with his life as Pharao's powerful minister of agriculture and his reunion with his father and his brothers. Toward the end of the second volume, he is thrown into the pit (he "dies"); toward the end of the third volume, he is once more thrown into the pit, a prison this time (he "dies" again). At the end of the first novel, his mother dies; at the end of the last, his father. According to the narrator, the fifth chapter of the last volume ("Tamar") is an "interpolation."

"Joseph" appears in the title of the tetralogy, in the titles of the second, third, and fourth volumes; it also is the first name mentioned (3)—six times in a paragraph and "with gratification" (4)—and the last one. Joseph is also the first, as well as the last, person in the tetralogy to speak.

The chapters and sections of the first novel are not always arranged chronologically. Jacob's return from Laban's place is narrated before his life there; Isaac's death before his blessing; Dinah's kidnaping before her birth. The chapter on Abraham in the second volume comes after eight chapters devoted to Jacob and Joseph. There is no transition between the section entitled "Benoni" and the preceding one, although they are four or five years apart. Nor is there a transition between the first and second chapters of *Young Joseph.* Indeed, the first chapter of *Young Joseph* takes place at the same time as the first chapter of *The Tales of Jacob,* or even slightly before. The Joseph story proper begins only with the third, or even fourth, chapter of the second volume.

Throughout the novel, there are continuous references to past and future happenings. The narration is frequently interrupted by passages that come close to being essays. Mann himself thought that many essays in *Joseph* did not belong into a novel and considered the third part to be more novelistic than the others because of the concentration on the erotic.

Mann's story of Joseph is perhaps sixty times as long as its biblical model, and the author was conscious of the fact that many readers would find that the original story could not be improved (667). Indeed some would, for instance, prefer the Bible's crisp, yet moving explanation "Jacob served seven years for Rachel and they seemed unto him but a few days for the love he had to her" to Mann's prolonged discussion of the nature of waiting and time. But Mann argues—tongue in cheek—that his work is "but a commentary," and that it comes closer to the richness of the original story as life itself told it than does the frightfully laconic tradition (667). Actually, the tetralogy only occasionally reads like a commentary, and its length derives less from Mann's scholarly readings than from his imagination, psychological interests, Realistic background, and intellectual playfulness. He has created new figures, enriched familiar ones with many new features, thoughts, and speeches, described temples, houses, gardens, cities, costumes, tools, food, festivals, etc., in great detail, and added vivid and moving scenes, although he—facetiously—denies being an "inventor of tales" (184).

The length and slowness of the narrative is bound to annoy some readers. In their very long dialogue, Peteprê's and Mut's thoughts are occasionally interpolated between their spoken words and are sometimes a page long (684, 702). Ruben thinks for forty-two lines during a conversation with Joseph (332). There are too many repetitions and too many speeches, it would seem to the general reader. Yet the author sometimes teasingly remarks that he only gives a sampling or a few examples (279, 614, 732, 740) and that he is constantly and necessarily practicing condensation (979 f.). Once he humorously voices his intention not to go into the details of Joseph's wedding feast because it would hurt Jacob's feelings, as if Jacob were alive and likely to read Mann's book; but then he gives the details anyway (1004-1007).

Some slips of the narrator may be traced to the length of the novel. In the beginning, he mentions that Jacob was to describe on his deathbed how the town of Harran suddenly loomed before him (146), but Jacob does nothing of the kind. Nor does Jacob "tell solemnly" how he "stood alone in the darkness of the bridal chamber," as the author anticipates (199).

The narrator continuously claims that his version of the story, as contrasted with all the others, is true, exact, objective, almost complete, and definitive, and that even the conversations, such as the first one between Peteprê and Joseph or between Pharao and Joseph, are rendered word for word. Only the unwary reader actually believes this assertion, which is meant humorously. Mann did not even believe that the patriarchs existed, and most of the book is his own invention.

Sometimes he stresses the fact that he is reporting something that former versions of the story have omitted (589) or that he goes to some length only to give the reader a clear picture

(872). He devotes whole pages to the question—not raised in the Bible but obviously interesting to a Realist—why Joseph, when he was sold, did not get in touch with his father or tell the Midianites about him (449 ff., 468 f.).

Occasionally he quotes the Bible verbatim (774, 1045). But his version often differs from the standard translation. For instance, he does not have Jacob make a special garment for Joseph, nor does he have the brothers take Joseph out of the well. At times he justifies his "correction" of the Bible, as in the question when Dinah was born (98) or how long Jacob served Laban (161). Once he corrects the German translation of the Bible (1166).

Certain numbers are strongly in evidence throughout the tetralogy. As in *The Magic Mountain,* the number seven is often used, particularly because it already plays an important part in the Bible. So does the number seventeen. No wonder, then, that each of the four volumes has seven chapters, and that the most moving chapter of the last book, containing the recognition scene, has seventeen sections. Because of Mann's number-concsciousness and number preferences, and also because he was humorously engaged in the parody of a Bible commentary, there are pages devoted to the number seventy, when seventy Israelites come to Egypt. The thirteen years between Joseph's entry into Egypt and his appearance before Pharao are arbitrarily divided by the author into seven (at Peteprê's), three (Mut's love), and three (in prison). "It could not be otherwise" (554). Because these numbers are neat, they are correct, the reader is told. It is also "more beautiful and more correct to have seven sons than eight" (1142).

Most trips last seventeen days or a multiple thereof. There are numerous humorous remarks about the years of plenty being five or seven in number. Joseph's having seven reasons for his chastity and three reasons for not being afraid of Pharao at his first encounter are other examples of Mann's play with numbers. Tamar is unique in more than one way: The folds between her brows have four meanings (1030), not three or five or seven.

Eliezer teaches Joseph about the properties of certain numbers. He omits the number forty, although it figures rather prominently in the Bible, and the Joseph tetralogy deals with forty years in Joseph's life, but forty is not a favorite number with Mann. According to the Bible, Jacob's body is treated for forty days by the embalmers. Mann makes it seventy.

Joseph and His Brothers is a stylistic as well as a narrative feast. Mann outdoes himself in beautifully constructed and cleverly involved sentences. The reader is greeted, almost at the very beginning, by a sentence which, in the German original, is more than forty-four lines long and includes a parenthesis of five lines (3, "Young Joseph. . ."). Like his perspective in time, the author's range of words is enormous. He plays with words and allusions, creates new compounds and dusts off old and forgotten words and usages. In his highly polished style, he sometimes uses obsolete double negatives as well as provocatively anachronistic new words, slang as well as regional expressions. There are numerous examples of groups of two, three, or four words held together by an alliteration, or a rhyme, or a pun, particularly in the last volume. Much of this playful artistry defies translation. One of the first word plays is that on the word "Ur." It is the country from which the original Abraham came but also a German prefix denoting oldest age or prime source, a prefix that fascinates young Castorp in *The Magic Mountain*.

Most of Mann's characters are skilled orators as well. Mut's style is called "literary" (744). In her "extraordinary speech" (708) to Dûdu, her well-turned phrases cover more than four pages. On his deathbed, Mont-kav makes a highly literary speech, which fills nine pages. One of Dûdu's statements exceeds two pages, including a parenthesis of five lines (712). Even eight-year old Benjamin can be articulate and mature (295, 297); and uncouth Laban, too, expresses himself in intricate speeches.

Because of the many "patterns," imitations, identifications, and correspondences, one could almost say that everything is a leitmotif, Mann's favorite stylistic device. As in his other works, the narrator or the reader ask many questions, sometimes rhetorical ones. Occasionally five questions follow each other (561, 668, 702). There are also numerous exclamations.

In *Joseph and His Brothers*, Mann in his own words, combines "myth and psychology." He fuses them with many other fields of human endeavor. He takes the archetypes and the collective unconscious from Jung, other psychological hypotheses from Freud, many facts and thoughts from works dealing with archeology, orientology, egyptology, comparative religion and mythology, Bible criticism, and from Arabic and Persian versions of the Joseph story. His interest in ancient Egypt and its mythology, incidentally, goes back to his childhood.

Mann's psychologized and humanized myth is mainly based on the ideas of "mythical identification" and of the Babylonian "rolling sphere," on Goethe's prototype, and on Nietzsche's "eternal return." Mann often describes as characteristic of the aging writer the shift of interest from the "bourgeois and individual" to the "mythical and typical." He uses "mythical" and "typical" as synonyms.

Man, as Thomas Mann affirms in the tetralogy as well as in his essays and letters, is much less of an individual than he wants or may want to be. His self is not entirely "shut up in its boundaries of flesh and time. Many of its elements belong to the world before it and outside of it" (78). Whether we know it or not, we must follow a certain pattern, "scheme," or prototype, we must walk in the well-marked footsteps of our predecessors and imitate them or identify ourselves with them. This is our prescribed "role" on earth, our destiny, and our character. Many of Mann's biblical figures are shown to fill out certain given forms, a mythical frame that was established by the fathers, or to regard experiences which actually were not theirs as belonging to their own life history. Again and again, the past becomes "present in the flesh," the "ego fades out and back into the archetype" (123), and the timeless present—an idea dear and familiar to Mann—is established. In the case of imitation, it is sometimes "difficult to tell whether it is the individual or the destiny that actually follows the pattern. The inward and outward play into each other" (551).

An extreme and slightly humorous case of this mythical identification and imitation is that of Eliezer. The original Eliezer was a son of the original Abraham born of a slave woman and later the head servant at Abraham's court. Throughout the centuries, Abraham's descendants had a servant named Eliezer. Jacob, Joseph's father, has one, too. He is Joseph's mentor. This Eliezer does not differ from the original Eliezer and often tells Joseph, for instance, how he had wooed Rebecca for Isaac. He uses the first instead of the third person because his ego is "not quite clearly demarcated, but opens at the back, as it were, and overflows into spheres external to his own individuality both in space and time" (78). Fittingly enough, Eliezer's features are so "tranquilly generalized and divinely inexpressive" that they suggest a mask (265).

Seemingly, these Biblical people "do not know who they are"; but they know perfectly well who they are, mythically and typically speaking. "Our present Esau" is another representative of a "timeless and extra-personal generalization" (124). As for the patriarchs, many an Abraham, Isaac, and Jacob made no clear distinction between their present and the present of former times and did not delineate their own individualities against the individualities of earlier Abrahams, Isaacs, and Jacobs (82).

Their mythical identification, akin to what anthropologists call "participation," gives the Biblical figures a feeling of security and dignity, though the role they have to play may be trivial, ridiculous or ugly. Even being rejected is a role like any other and has its own dignity (1189). The sureness and dignity derive from the consciousness that one is once more presenting something legitimate and traditional.

When traders enrich themselves, it is to conform to their role on this earth (523-524). Though they are tricked out of things that rightfully belong to them, Laban as well as Esau play their roles with "more or less awareness and consent" (245). When Laban is so clumsy in his search that he smears his beard with green dye, it is only because he is conscious that to be ridiculous is his role in life, and because he is eager to play this role well (246). When some of his brothers want to kill Joseph, it is only because it fits their role best. At the end, Joseph forgives his brothers because they "were cast in the villain's part" (1207).

Because of the "revolving sphere," the boundaries of a man's fate and self are fluid or open, not only toward his predecessors or ancestors but also toward the gods. There is a heavenly and an earthly hemisphere which complement each other in such a way that what is above is also below, and what happens in the earthly sphere repeats itself in the heavenly sphere and has a starry prototype or counterpart. But the sphere also rolls, so that the heavenly can turn into the earthly, the earthly into the heavenly (124, 389). Gods may become men, men may become gods and later men again. The question what Osiris was in the beginning, whether god or man, remains unanswered, since there is no beginning in the rolling sphere (125). In Abraham that which had previously been celestial became flesh; his wandering was the earthly reflection and imitation of the wandering of the moon (1140). He supported himself upon the divine also when he scattered the robbers from beyond the Euphrates (282). When Eliezer covered a distance, which it takes twenty days to traverse, in just three days, because the earth "sprang to meet him," he must have had a winged hat and winged feet like Hermes, Mann's favorite god.

Imitation and identification, therefore, extend to gods. The course of his life appears to Jacob in the light of cosmic correspondences. There is an ascension (the great vision at Bethel), a descent into hell (his trip to Laban's), a sly and silly devil (Laban), and an Ishtar (Rachel).

Joseph takes advantage of mythological thinking by often consciously playing a part that suggests something divine, and thus startling or dazzling everybody. He is greatly helped by Mann, who playfully arranges events and situations so that Joseph may appear as a reincarnation or prefiguration of a god. Joseph is a born impersonator like Felix Krull, an artistic and enthusiastic player of many parts. First he consciously and unconsciously suggests the beautiful and torn god, the Sumerian Tammuz, or the Syrian Adonis. In Egypt he aptly represents Osiris. Later, as a shrewd mediator and provider, he is a new Hermes. In his dealings with Petepré's wife, he also is a new Gilgamesh. Because of his precaution, he is a new Noa, or Noa's Babylonian counterpart Utnapishtim (981); and later on, at the height of his glory, he is an incarnation of a Nile divinity, of the bull Hapi (1164). He also prefigures Christ in many ways. His frequent answer "I am it," which impresses his interrogators, is a formula used by a god in disclosing his identity.

This psychologized mythology or mythical psychology satisfies Mann's appreciation of tradition and continuity as well as his sense of role-playing. Since man is acting out his prescribed role on earth, he becomes an actor. Joseph is a better, wittier, and more calculating player than anybody. It is this playing for his own sake, this egotistical play with allusions and "many forms of imitation" (551) which Jacob blames Joseph for.

[51]

The sphere not only revolves but apparently also progresses. The heavenly and earthly "patterns" and "schemes" change slowly and in the direction of the good. Jacob and Joseph, for instance, are not killed by their hostile brothers, as Abel was by Cain. Isaac is not sacrificed by his father, as first-born sons used to be, and as Laban's son was. The change of patterns is an important factor in the tetralogy's view of religion.

In *Joseph and His Brothers*, religion is defined in different ways. It is, first of all and in line with an old thought of Mann's, "Frömmigkeit" (piety), the reverence toward death. "Frömmigkeit" later takes on the meaning of "concentration upon the self and its salvation." This subjectivism, however, does not mean isolation or a callous disregard of the supra-personal. For if "Frömmigkeit" means being concerned with the importance of the self, then "Feierlichkeit" (solemnity), its cognate, means the extension of the self into the eternal. "Feierlichkeit" enhances the dignity of the self ("Würde") to the point of "Weihe" (consecration, 1139).

One notices Mann's predilection for alliteration in connection with the subject of religion. Alliteration of religious significance is also used by Peteprê's parents: "heilig"—"herrlich" (holy—splendid, "herrlich" being also a pun on "Herr," gentleman and Lord). "Heilig" stands for the old, for woman, for the earth; "herrlich," for the new, for man or heaven. Out of concern that their marriage might no longer be in accordance with the new spirit, Peteprê's parents Huia and Tuia, brother and sister, emasculate their baby son. While this action is grievously wrong, their basic concern was right and identical with Abraham's, Jacob's or Pharao's anxiousness about God and His change. According to many passages in Mann's later essays and letters, religion is also attentiveness to the new, to the change in the "world spirit" and obedience to this change.

Customs that once were sacred, such as sacrificing the first-born, become an abomination (587). When the old is rotted with age, it is honorable only in appearance, but is in fact an abomination and indecency before the Lord, says Joseph. In spite of all the "patterns," "footsteps," prototypes, repetitions, and imitations, there is change in the world, and there must be a corresponding change in man. There is nothing more exciting and more important in the world, Peteprê's father says, than being concerned about the order of the day and the new era (579-580).

Abraham "discovers" God; he is, so to speak, God's father. As God was anxious to make His name great, Abraham did a good deed, since he made ready the way of His realization in the mind of man (283-284). God and man need each other, help each other, and become holy in each other. But it is characteristic of Mann's diffidence toward mysticism, and somewhat inconsistent with his remarks on "Feierlichkeit," that Abraham's ego is not at all willing to be lost in God and thus to be one with Him (287).

Contrary to the Bible, God does not play an active part in the tetralogy. He is but the object of thoughts, stories, dreams, and songs. Mann is reluctant to use the supernatural in a natural story, as he implies when he ventures the "guess" that God might have shown Joseph to Mont-kav in a favorable light (535). After the publication of the first volume, he, therefore, found that the supernatural "man in the field" who takes Joseph to his brothers, then guards Joseph's "tomb," and later leads the Ismaelites to Egypt—and who is but an angel in disguise— was not aesthetically justified. He felt as uneasy about the appearance of this angel as about the apparition of Joachim in a World War I steel helmet in *The Magic Mountain*.

There is a rational or psychological, rather than a sentimental or mystical element in this religion of attentiveness to the new spirit. One has to be "skilled in the dealing with God" (514). It is "Gottesklugheit," good judgment directed toward God. Sin is a mistake, a folly, a clumsy blunder against this good judgment (469, 855). There is nothing more religious than to study God's "soul life."

Mann delights in showing connections and parallels between the different mythologies and religions. He particularly christianizes the Jewish religion. Salvation, for instance—which is often mentioned—is not a Jewish concern; and at the time of the partriarchs the Jews did not think of a savior. Nor did they ever believe, as Jacob does, in a trinity (Father, Shepherd, Angel). There are parallels to Christ's life in Abraham's childhood and in Joseph's life ("virgin birth," "lamb," three days in the "tomb," being sold for money, being kissed by Judah). Joseph also thinks that God must become man and bear man's guilt.

The tetralogy stresses the "fluidity of boundaries and the unity of the world" (908), so that, for instance, politics cannot be separated from religion and art, contrary to the view held by Mann in his *Reflections of a Non-Political Man*. "For with the world-whole and its unity the human being has always and ever to do, whether he knows it or not" (909).

This unity sometimes is a "unity of the double." It means, for instance, the "exchangeability of above and below." The double does not play any significant role in Jacob's religion. And still he yields to its ancient mighty spell and knows nothing sweeter (1194). Mann, too, yields to its spell. He is intrigued by the double sense of past and future in the phrase "once upon a time" and frequently mentions the double blessing, not only in connection with Joseph. Probably influenced by Freud's belief in the basic bisexuality of man, and by remarks of ethnologists, anthropologists, and Jung that it was frequently held to be a divine or ideal state, Mann stresses the bisexuality of divine or ideal figures.

God himself is "Baal and Baalat at one and the same time" (288). Ishtar, as well as her lover Tammuz, are bisexual (305). "Double-sexedness is consummate. The double-sexed powers unite both male and female glory in themselves; like the image of the Nile with one woman's breast and one man's; or like the moon that was wife to the sun and yet male to the earth" (588). Art, too, is male as well as female (596), a thought often expressed by Mann. The sex of the Egyptian king is double (946); he is the father and mother of the countries. Israel is the bride and the bridegroom of God (305). After Rachel's death, Jacob is Joseph's father and mother (435), he is "double, Jacob and Rachel" (1194). Joseph, on the other hand, is also Rachel to Jacob.

In spite of Mann's avowed turn from the individual toward the "typical," few figures in the tetralogy are as inexpressive as Eliezer. Some are highly individualized and interesting. Some are created after living models. Many faces and figures, including those of minor characters, are described in great detail. The two lines devoted to Peteprê's navel may be a record of sorts (682).

Jacob stands out because of his constant anxiousness about God's intentions and his immense love of his "true wife" and "true son." For all his tenderness, his sons see in him a "father-tyrant" (1185). His spiritual, solemn, and perhaps tragic grandeur matches, or more than matches, Joseph's physical, social and intellectual greatness, enormous wit, cheer, and charm. One may sometimes feel that the tetralogy could well have been called *Jacob and His Sons*. When Jacob dies, the book ends, or very nearly does so.

Joseph's brothers are each marked by a dominant character trait, which they retain to old age, often with humorous effect. Judah, perhaps the most interesting among them, shows some leadership and, in spite of, or because of, the constant fight with his flesh, of his defeats, and of his guilt feelings, eventually inherits the spiritual blessing, which at least in Jacob's mind greatly outweighs Joseph's worldly double blessing.

The eunuch Peteprê, a colossus of flesh, is an extreme example of what Mann calls "formal" or "representative" existence. He is a titular captain of Pharao's guard, a titular commandant of the royal prisons, without wielding any power. Of course, he is also a titular husband. But he is a very intelligent, sensitive and just person, even though he "stands outside of humanity" (872).

Pharao, Amenhotep IV, is a decadent, ecstatic, sick man, who wants to found a universal, supra-national religion based on love and the veneration of an invisible god Atôn.

Beknechons, his opposite and Amun's high priest, bears a striking resemblance to Mussolini, with his chin thrust up and out, his impressive head, his fervent nationalism, and his troops who are separate from the royal army.

The modest and likable Mont-kav, Peteprê's steward, is certainly drawn as an individual; the symptoms and the treatment of his kidney ailment are described extensively.

Mai Sachme, the calm prison warden, later Joseph's friend and steward, who is also a physician and a writer, is created after Martin Gumpert, a friend of Thomas Mann, who had Mai Sachme's facial features and was also a writer and physician. As Joseph takes Mai Sachme into his story—a fact which is repeatedly mentioned—Mann brought Gumpert into his. There may be some reason why Mai Sachme has the same name as Mut's father.

Mann wanted to "rehabilitate" Mut, Peteprê's aristocratic wife. He actually rehabilitated her sexual desire by showing its intensity, its power of transformation—it eventually transforms a "moon nun" into a witch—, its anguish, and frustration. While Mut, the female protagonist of the third volume, is the articulate, inventive, and suffering representative of frustrated sexual love (her seductive white arms recall those of Clavdia), Rachel, the female heroine of the first volume, is the epitome of "true" and moving marital love, including some of its frustrations.

Tamar, the strange and powerful feminine protagonist of the last volume, marries two men and, when they die, prostitutes herself in order to "interpolate" herself into the history of the "spiritual tribe" and become the ancestress of the promised savior.

On the grotesque side are the two dwarfs, Bes, the helpful one, and Dûdu, the scheming, nationalistic one (who continuously boasts of his virility), as well as Peteprê's unwise and wisened parents Huia and Tuia. In German, Huia and Tuia are called Huij and Tuij, names probably suggested by "pfui," since the parents did something disgusting to their baby boy.

Joseph stands for many, perhaps too many things. He is, first of all, an ideal figure. Especially in his youth, he is a synthesis of beauty and spirit, such as is ordinarily not to be found in human life. In later years he represents another admirable synthesis, which "reveals the deepest depth of his nature and is almost Joseph himself"; almost, because nobody can ever tell with certainty what he really is—or so the scribe Khamat asserts. He is "tâm," combining the positive and the negative: piety, which is reverence toward death and the past ("Frömmigkeit"), and friendliness toward life ("Freundlichkeit").

Feeling for death by itself makes for rigidity and gloom; feeling for life by itself for flat mediocrity and dull-wittedness. Where veneration for death is moderated by friendliness to life, life acquires depth and poignancy, and wit and sympathy arise. This is Joseph's double blessing, which was bestowed on him from the heights above and the depths which lie beneath (996).

Joseph is something of an artist. He has the poet's sensitivity and mastery of words, the actor's enjoyment of, and skill in, playing roles. Toward the end of the tetralogy he is the co-author, stage manager, and principal actor of an important episode in his life. Like Felix Krull's, his roles, talents, and achievements are theoretically unlimited.

He is also an impudent impersonator and rogue, far more of a *Hochstapler* than Felix Krull. In many ways, he is meant to correspond to Hermes, the patron god of cheats and liars. His life story often reads like a picaresque novel.

The magic of his person, his many talents, as well as his getting stout in middle age and later losing weight, remind one of Goethe. Joseph is also slapped on the back by Pharao, as Goethe was by the duke of Weimar. He obviously conforms to Goethe's advice "stirb und werde." With his shrewdness, power, popularity, charm, sympathy, economic and political "new deal," he also "is" F. D. Roosevelt.

In some respects, he "is" also Thomas Mann or the ideal Mann had of himself. He is a superb master of irony ("wit") and ambiguity, and thinks that serenity ("Heiterkeit") and artful jest are the best things in life (1056). He delights in allusions and correspondences and is a living synthesis of generally irreconcilable opposites. Like Thomas Mann, he was born in June before the summer solstice at noon (67, 357). He is a late comer, too, and different from his ancestors, more refined, more educated, more complex. The hostility that existed between Thomas Mann and his less renowned older brother Heinrich Mann and their reconciliation a year or so before Thomas Mann started the Joseph story suggests another similarity between Mann and Joseph himself, and may have provided a stimulus for the whole work. Benjamin, incidentally, has some features of Mann's much younger brother Viktor.

That Joseph finds his way from the "artistic egocentricity" of his youth, as Mann puts it, to social consciousness parallels Mann's development, too. Mann declared in a lecture on *Joseph and His Brothers* that in Joseph the opposition of artist and bourgeois, individual and community is overcome. But the social conscience in Joseph is not basic; he is socially committed, but with reservations. He devotes his great talents to the country, not because he wants to help his fellow men in an emergency but because, under the circumstances, this is the only possible way of playing a role, his role. Similarly, before he becomes a provider, he decides to help Peteprê, but only, or mostly, because this would help him, too (588).

As Mann explains, Joseph the Provider is socially "a bit more mature, but to play with the myth, to play in general is still the main thing for him."[1] Throughout his life, Joseph cannot desist from playing (853). His social role is only a means and a mask. He is neither a true Egyptian nor a true member of the Israelite tribe. With all his friendliness, he remains set apart. He does not really care about Egypt (990), but there is also a marked gulf between him and his father (1174), whom he does not see very often.

While the others have but one traditional name, which, on occasion, they discard in order to take on somebody else's (Eliezer), Joseph has a great many names, though at one time he has none at all, and literally makes a name for himself; but his name does not become that of a tribe. This parallels his many talents and roles and his unique status as a genius.

Joseph and His Brothers is Mann's longest, most optimistic, most charming and most tender novel. One senses how greatly he enjoyed writing it. But the enjoyment of some readers may be somewhat dampened by its length, its "secularization" of religion, its display of erudition, and its overly intricate sentences.

CHAPTER 5

The Old Genius and His Old Beloved

THE BELOVED RETURNS (*Lotte in Weimar*) first appeared in successive issues of the magazine *Maß und Wert* in 1938 and 1939 and was published in book form in 1939, i.e., between the third and the fourth volumes of the *Joseph* novel. It is concerned with Charlotte Kestner, who comes to the little German town of Weimar in September, 1816, ostensibly to visit her sister but actually to see the world-famous man, now sixty-seven years old, who courted her forty-four years ago: Goethe, Germany's greatest writer. Charlotte immediately becomes a center of attraction, for she is the original Lotte in Goethe's most popular book, *The Sorrows of Young Werther*. She is accompanied by an unmarried daughter and a maid.

On her first day in Weimar, Charlotte is visited in the inn "Zum Elephant" by four people. First, Rose Cuzzle, an Irishwoman who has done portraits of many famous personalities, sketches her. Then Dr. Riemer, Goethe's secretary, engages her in a discussion about Goethe and the nature of genius. Later, the young, articulate, and homely Adele Schopenhauer, sister of the philosopher, asks Charlotte to use her "maternal status" in the Goethe family to prevent Adele's friend Ottilie von Pogwisch from marrying August, Goethe's only son. Finally, August himself arrives and, at the end of a long conversation about his father and himself, communicates to Charlotte his father's invitation for dinner in a "small circle" to be given three days from now. Then, in a brief flashback, we witness Goethe's activities of that same day—his thoughts and feelings from the moment he awakens, thinking about his dream, dictating to his secretaries, having breakfast, washing, being shaved, making plans for the day and his works, and reminiscing—up to the time he asks his son to invite Charlotte. We then witness the dinner at Goethe's house. A few weeks later, Charlotte views a performance of the work of a minor dramatist from Goethe's box at the local theater, and, returning to the inn in Goethe's carriage, she has an imaginary conversation with a vision of Goethe.

Clearly, this "novel," as Thomas Mann has called it, is neither a novel, as most readers understand the term, nor, with its more than four hundred pages, a novella. The general characteristics of the work, with its slow-moving development, its direct and indirect quotations from passages in Goethe's works, letters, and conversations, and its predominance of monologues, dialogues, and general discussions over narration defy definition.

It consists of nine chapters. Chapter VII is singled out; while the other chapters are simply labelled Chapter I, II, III, and so forth, it is called *the* seventh chapter. The reason is obvious: It is the longest chapter and contains Goethe's interior monologue, or rather a succession of interior monologues, the first one being fourteen pages long. Chapter V is the only one with a title ("Adele's Story"). Goethe appears only in the last three chapters—in the last one as a phantom—but he dominates the other chapters, too. A lot is said about, for, and against him in the preceding ones.

The novel has a circular structure. It begins and ends with Mager greeting Lotte, as she alights from a carriage. The situation is the same yet quite different, since Lotte has learned a great deal about Goethe in the meantime, and Mager's attitude toward her has changed considerably, too. There is a certain irony in this circularity.

Goethe, it is well known, not only dominates Mann's novel but also German literature. Thomas Mann, of course, read Goethe in school; and in one of his earliest novellas, "Disillusionment" (1896), he quotes a paragraph from the *Sorrows of Young Werther* (26). He later often compared his own *Buddenbrooks* with *Werther*, since both were greatly successful first novels of young men about twenty-six years of age. His interest and delight in Goethe increased in the course of time. Old Goethe's pathetic but undignified love for the seventeen-year old Ulrike von Levetzow in the Bohemian resort of Marienbad prefigures Gustav Aschenbach's pathetic love for young Tadzio in the Italian resort of the Lido. After writing the *Magic Mountain,* he was attracted by Goethe to the extent that he often felt united with him in a *unio mystica.* He wrote about ten essays on Goethe, chief among them "Goethe and Tolstoy." In some respects Joseph, too, resembles Goethe. *Felix Krull* is, to a certain degree, a parody of Goethe's novel *Wilhelm Meister* as well as of Goethe's poetic autobiography *Dichtung und Wahrheit.* But by far the largest monument to Mann's interest in Goethe and to his frequent identification with him is *The Beloved Returns.*

In this novel, a favorite theme of Thomas Mann's writing, the conflict between art and life, returns. Art, of course, is represented by Goethe and life by Charlotte Kestner, the intelligent, practical, and resolute mother of nine. She returns to see Goethe again, because a feeling of uneasiness about the strange way in which she was wooed and deserted by the young poet has never left her. This feeling was more tantalizing than the annoyance about the fact that Goethe publicized his relationship to her in his novel; and it was greater than the satisfaction of having been immortalized. Her uneasiness and apprehension, however, are only sharpened during her stay in Weimar, and particularly during the dinner. Only at the very end they are dissolved by Goethe's vague and conciliatory words. Her head shakes because of her age, but one cannot help wondering whether her disapproval of the situation which she encounters in Goethe's stately house does not intensify the shaking. The historical Lotte Kestner actually visited Weimar in 1816, but most likely not for the reason Mann attributes to her.

As in "Death in Venice," and particularly in *Doctor Faustus,* Mann intends to show the shortcomings and transgressions of the great artist. He is very far from the almost unquestioning admiration and awe in which Goethe is generally held in Germany. The Olympian sometimes even seems to be hauled down from Mount Olympus to be displayed with his human, all-too-human, or even inhuman, traits. According to Lotte, young Goethe was a "parasite." He only courted her because she already was engaged; and he was sure that he would not be tied down and would not have to assume any responsibility. He only looked for experiences to be used in his writings and thus, in his own words (318), "betrayed" love and life and human beings to art.

When, in the interior monologue, Goethe's attention wanders to *Werther*, he hardly thinks of the real Lotte (318 ff.). When his son tells him that his beloved of forty-four years ago has returned, he is barely interested, slightly annoyed, repeatedly brushes off the topic, and grudgingly accords Lotte the standard treatment for important guests. "Why could not the old woman have spared me this?" (371). His coldness and aloofness are also seen in his relationship to his mother, whom he had not seen for eleven years before she died, and in his attitude toward Schiller, whom he admired and who helped him greatly in his writing, but whom he actually disliked. No true friendship is apparent; the many cordial relations which the young Goethe entertained are hardly mentioned. At the dinner, the "beloved" has to address him as "Your Excellency." Not only is the Goethe of the last chapter a ghost, but there is something unreal and ghostlike in his other appearances as well, and that in spite of the many details of his face, voice, and behavior which are adduced. While in "Tonio Kröger" and in "Death in Venice" Mann shows how art destroys, to some extent, the warm human life and the happiness in the artist himself, in "Tristan," *Doctor Faustus*, and *The Beloved Returns* one sees how it destroys the happiness and lives of those who serve or love the artist.

One reason for the uncanniness which Lotte feels, therefore, is the "smell of sacrifice" that surrounds Goethe. She maintains again and again that one should not sacrifice one's existence for anybody or anything, but lead a full life, as she had done. She blames her own daughter for wasting her life by taking care of her invalid brother. As she finds out, there are quite a few people who have sacrificed, or are sacrificing, their lives to Goethe's genius. There is young Friederike Brion, the daughter of an Alsatian clergyman, whom he deserted after a few months of seemingly ardent love, and who had pined away her life. There is Dr. Riemer, a learned man who might have had a successful academic career, but who has almost given up his own ego to put himself into Goethe's place in order to be able to write as Goethe might have done. Unlike Charlotte, he maintains that everybody was not born to lead his own life; but he is perhaps only rationalizing his own situation, from which he suffers.

There is Goethe's son August, who has no will of his own, who ignominiously had to stay away from the army because his father wanted it that way, and who is going to marry Ottilie because this somehow fits into his father's scheme. When, at the end, Lotte disapprovingly mentions the "sacrifices to his greatness," Goethe philosophically replies: "Transformation is all. They sacrificed to the god, and in the end the sacrifice was God . . . I, first and last, am the sacrifice and he that offers it." While it pacifies Lotte, mainly because she wants to be pacified, it does not sound altogether convincing.

The great artist has some of the attitudes of every great man. He tyrannizes the company he is in, imposes his whims and interests on everybody, degrades people to become sycophants or echoes. When Goethe tells his dinner guests about the Chinese saying "The great man is a national misfortune," they laugh boisterously, but Lotte does not join in the laughter. She feels cold and is afraid that somebody might jump up and shout: "The Chinese are right." Goethe does not like to oppress people, he tells his son, but that is what he actually does. He knows that they all will heave a sigh of relief when he dies. Almost from the start, Lotte senses in Riemer "a certain rebellion against Goethe's greatness" (78).

Riemer, who divests himself of his own self, in order to be able to serve his master well, says some of the most damaging things about Goethe. He blames him for a "peculiar coldness," a destructive equanimity (82), nihilism, an all-embracing irony, puckishness, a Protean inclination toward constant self-transformation, frequent sullenness and stiffness, for recklessness, breach of faith, and a lack of enthusiasm.

Lotte, too, is quite aware of certain negative aspects of Goethe's personality. When he was in love with her, she sensed in the young Goethe something "unreal, irresponsible." Later she calls him a creature "inhuman, without purpose or poise" (31), a phrase taken from Goethe's *Faust*. One of old Goethe's stories at the dinner party "chills and frightens" her (423). Another story makes her "blush up to the roots of her crown of grey hair," and she sits in terror lest her host might expand further on his story. The narrator himself speaks of the childlike vacillation, coquettishness, and ambiguity that could be seen in Goethe's features.

The repeated reference to Goethe's physical defects, to his rheumatism and stiffness, for instance, to his frequent grave illnesses, and to his immoderate eating and drinking also tends to dim Goethe's lustre.

In spite of all his negative features and the suspicions and fears of his environment, Goethe's greatness shines brilliantly throughout the novel. Mann succeeded in communicating his unbelievably wide range of interests, ideas, and activities, the depth of his insight, his sensitivity, his periodic rejuvenation, his vitality, and the beauty of his features. Again and again the comparison with a god is drawn. And while Lotte is repelled by the odor of sacrifice that surrounds Goethe, Riemer, a grudging admirer of Goethe, speaks of the divine odor emanating from him. While she calls the young Goethe a parasite, Riemer speaks of "parasitism which is of the god" (110). One of the advantages of the interior monologue, of which Mann has fully availed himself, is precisely the possibility of showing the intellectual and emotional richness of a person. One gets an intimation of Goethe's interests or achievements in literature, the arts, meteorology, administration, geology, the theater, politics, physics, architecture, botany, and so on.

An important theme of the novel is that of repetition and return. Thus, Goethe's love affairs, in spite of all the distinguishing features, are repetitions of the same episode, namely the encounter with Friederike Brion. Ottilie, Goethe's prospective daughter-in-law, is another Charlotte Buff or Lili Schönemann; the triangle Willemer—Marianne—Goethe is but a repetition of the triangle Kestner—Charlotte—Goethe. The similarity between August and his father is an attempt of life at repeating itself. The *Divan*, a recent collection of Orient-inspired poems, is the old *Werther* in a different costume and on a higher level.

Repetition is intensification and spiritualization. Experience itself is weak, it has to be relived. The never-ending circle conquers death. For all the constant changes and transformations, there is a basic unity in the universe and in history.

Some of the ideas expressed in the novel are probably less characteristic of the Goethe of 1816 than of the Mann of 1938. One of them is the allusion to psychoanalysis, whose founder, Freud, was greatly admired and celebrated by Mann, shortly before publication of *The Beloved Returns*, in an important essay, "Freud and the Future" (1936): From the study of the pathological there will come the boldest advances into the darkness of life (334).

Another idea which Mann often repeated after he had given up the non-political stand of his younger years is that politics is connected with everything. The totality of human existence, true humanism, is unthinkable without an active interest in politics. "In a hundred ways it is indissoluble from one's views, one's religion, one's convictions. It is a factor in everything—bound up with the ethical, the aesthetic, with things apparently intellectual and philosophic" (266).

Mann's anger about the great following that Nazism found in Germany and about its disastrous consequences is manifest in the passages which chastise the Germans. There are allusions to Hitler, to the Nazi plans for world conquest, and to the impending catastrophe of World War II (330-331, 338). In accordance with Mann's thoughts in the middle twenties and the *Magic Mountain*, Goethe thinks that the role of Germany should lie in mediation.

Another of Mann's ideas expressed by Goethe is that of "entering in contact" with the raw material before writing creatively. Indirectly describing Mann's extensive use of "sources," his Goethe remarks: "Contact, good word, expresses how you bore and burrow into some beautiful new world you have seized upon, dig away like possessed, till you know its secrets and can speak its tongue. And nobody sees the difference between imitated and invented detail" (336).

Lotte in Weimar itself is a case in point. It is often difficult to decide whether a remark or an event is historical or fictional. At any rate, Mann's knowledge of Goethe's life and his works is extraordinary. Many of the quotations, variations, and allusions, however, are lost on the reader who happens not to be a Goethe philologist. More of the allusions and references, of course, are lost in translation.

Naturally, the vast scholarship is not served up by Mann in a pedantic or pedestrian way. Many characters are vividly drawn, the places are sharply delineated, and anecdotes enliven the conversation. Irony, that necessary salt, as Mann's Goethe declares, pervades much of the book. And there are many touches of humor. The pompous head waiter Mager with his pretensions to culture, Lotte's idea of seeing Goethe in the pale pink dress with the missing bow to remind him of her youth, her jealousy of the other women in his life, the female literary clubs, the curiosity and gossiping which prevail in Weimar are examples of Mann's humorous vein.

Everybody seems to speak in the very formal and dry style of the old Goethe and to master the art of dialectics. Mann even made a point of suggesting the period through certain peculiarities in language and spelling. Goethe's five internal monologues do not really break the literary tradition. Although they are based on free association, they do not run wild. The associations are not utterly loose and irresponsible daydreams, but largely controlled by somebody who is anxious to control his feelings and thoughts and to organize the day that has just begun and his life, which is nearing its end. Sentence structure and punctuation are normal. Above all, the associations cannot really be "free," since much of their content is historical. An objection to these monologues may either come from people who think it presumptuous or sacrilegious, even for a Thomas Mann, to pretend to enter into the innermost recesses of Goethe's mind or from readers who look in a novel for fiction rather than facts.

While the mythical *Joseph* tetralogy is, to some extent, an answer to the shabby and dangerous myths of Nazism, to its anti-Semitism, narrow nationalism and adoration of power, the historical *Beloved Returns,* with its stress on the autonomous and free individual, on the fully developed, truly great personality, on culture, and tolerance is another answer to Nazism, to its barbarism, intolerance, and its rigid mass society. Above all, however, it is, in spite of all the blemishes in the Goethe image, Mann's finest and most elaborate tribute to a personality which has fascinated and inspired him for decades. Like Joseph, Goethe was to Thomas Mann an ideal, almost a divine figure. Goethe, too, had Joseph's double blessing, that of nature and of spirit (83).

For all its craftsmanship and its wealth of ideas, Mann's Goethe novel does not rank among his best works; it is too slow and too cluttered with learned details and allusions. Very few would subscribe to Stefan Zweig's enthusiastic assertion that it is Mann's "most perfect masterpiece."[1]

CHAPTER 6

Music, Germany and the Devil

IN 1942, while still working on *Joseph*, Mann started his reading of sources of another novel; and in May of 1943, he began writing *Doctor Faustus: The Life of the German Composer Adrian Leverkühn as Told by a Friend*. It is amazing that Mann's most somber novel followed his most optimistic one after an interval of less than five months. In his last composition, a song of woe, the fictitious composer Leverkühn intends to take back Beethoven's ode to joy, and it is as if Mann himself, in *Doctor Faustus*, intended to take back the cheer and hope of his own *Joseph*.

Mann went back forty years to the time when he wrote *Buddenbrooks*, "Tristan," and "Tonio Kröger." He dug up some old papers containing literary motifs and plans, particularly a three-line plan of a book on Doctor Faustus. At that time, he already thought of writing about an artist's pact with the devil and about the liberating effect of syphilis on creative power.

We are fairly well informed about the origin of *Doctor Faustus*, since two years after the publication of the novel, Mann published a book about it. In this *Story of a Novel: The Genesis of Doctor Faustus*, he does what Serenus Zeitblom, the imaginary narrator of the novel, does: he devotes a number of pages to the War and to its disastrous effects on Germany. It is the grief about the great destruction of human lives and cultural values, about the social, political, and economic collapse of his beloved country that is responsible for the tragic mood of *Doctor Faustus*. The last two words of the novel are "fatherland" and "end." The last two works of the composer Leverkühn are about an end: his *Apocalypse* about the end of the world, and his *Lamentation of Doctor Faustus* about the end of the old magician and, symbolically, his own death. The preceding chapters of the book, too, "attempt to paint the final stage of a society and to conjure up the feeling of the end in every sense" (*Story*, 131).

But *Doctor Faustus* is not only a "Lamentation of Dr. Mann" about the end of his country. It is also a bitter accusation against his country, which, like the old Faustus and the new composer Leverkühn, signed a contract in blood and sold its soul to the devil. Thus Mann joins the other great German writers who severely censured their country and their countrymen: Hölderlin, Goethe, Heine, Platen, Nietzsche, and Hesse. But *Doctor Faustus* is self-accusation, too. Mann never made a distinction between a good and a bad Germany. He thought—and Zeitblom also expresses this view—that some of the evil characteristics that brought the scourge of Nazism to Germany and the world, to some extent, had been manifest at all times in every German, including the greatest ones (482).

This self-accusation for political or non-political opinions held in the past is coupled with personal confessions. Old and painful secrets are finally revealed or hinted at. Since the confession is made in fictional form, in ambiguities, allusions, or exaggerations, the reader can only guess the nature of these secrets.

While *Royal Highness, The Magic Mountain, Joseph,* and *Felix Krull* were originally planned as novellas, Mann always thought of *Doctor Faustus* as a novel, more specifically, as a novel of his country, his time, and his life, "disguised in the story of a sinful artist." For this ambitious project he consulted books about music and musicians, about theology, medicine, and history; he read Kierkegaard, Reinhold Niebuhr, the old German chapbook of Doctor Faustus, Marlowe's *Doctor Faustus*, Grimmelshausen's *Simplizissimus,* works by and on Luther, by and on Nietzsche, books on Hutten and Tilman Riemenschneider, and studied some of Dürer's paintings.

His work, an expression and revival of mental anguish, drained much of his strength. It was hampered by sickness and travels, interrupted by a lung cancer operation, and finished in 1947. After more than forty pages had been eliminated at the advice of Mann's daughter Erika, the novel was still around 770 pages long, i.e., about one third of *Joseph.* Mann rightly called it his "wildest" book, while the preceding biblical tetralogy might be called his most civilized one.

Born in 1885, Adrian Leverkühn spends the first ten years of his life on the family farm at Buchel in Thuringia. His father, a "dreamer and speculator," is fascinated by weird phenomena in nature, the fluidity of boundaries between the inorganic and the organic, and between animal and plant life. For nine years, Adrian is a brilliant student at a *Gymnasium* in nearby Kaisersaschern-on-the-Saale, a fictitious town. There Serenus Zeitblom, son of a local pharmacist and two years older than Adrian, is his schoolmate. Kretzschmar, a stuttering organist, becomes his mentor. For about two years he studies theology at the University of Halle and then, for almost five years, music at the University of Leipzig, where he obtains his doctorate in 1910. In 1906, he willfully contracts syphilis. In Palestrina, Italy, he engages in a "conversation" with the devil. In 1913, he settles on the farm of the Schweigestills at Pfeiffering, from where he occasionally takes trips to nearby Munich. Times of insufferable headaches and of extreme euphoria alternate. He has a few understanding and admiring friends, publishers, and critics, but the general reaction to his music is hostile; it is felt to be cold parody. In 1930, he becomes insane and is taken by his mother back to Buchel, where he dies in 1940. His compositions consist of an impressionist symphonic phantasy called "Ocean Lights," various songs, an opera based on Shakespeare's *Love's Labor's Lost*, an ironic symphony, "Marvels of the Universe," an operatic suite for the puppet theater after medieval stories, a violin concerto, some chamber music, and two oratorios, *Apocalypsis cum figuris,* after woodcuts by Dürer, and *Lamentation of Dr. Faustus.*

Zeitblom, who has almost always been very close to him, has studied classical philology, was a professor at a *Gymnasium* in Kaisersaschern, and taught from about 1912 at Freising in Bavaria. He resigned in 1933, because of his opposition to the Third Reich.

It is an illustration of Mann's customary play with numbers that Adrian spends his first and his last ten years—his first and his second childhood—at Buchel, and that his stay at Pfeiffering, the most productive period of his life, lasts seventeen years. There are a few cases of oversight in the arrangement of dates. Adrian goes to Leipzig in 1905 according to one assertion (136), and in 1906 according to another (8). Either date is corroborated or gainsaid by other facts in Adrian's life. Zeitblom takes up his position in Freising in 1912, according to one passage (10), and in 1913 according to another (261).

There is not much action proper to be found in *Doctor Faustus.* Leverkühn lives at the edge or outside of society and political events and shuns friendship and love. His encounter with the devil, patterned after Ivan's experience in Dostoevsky's *Brothers Karamasoff*, is a hallucination. His excursion into the depths of the sea is but a fantasy based on scientific readings. The few trips he takes are professional. They are devoted to work or to listening to music rather than to personal experiences or to relaxation or education. The strange trip he takes to meet the prostitute seems to form an exception; but it, too, is connected with his work.

Neither the long description of the music store in Kaisersaschern, nor Kretzschmar's lectures and those of the theology professors Kumpf and Schleppfuβ, nor the vaporous discussions of the theology students make for exciting reading. The Munich society stories are novelistic in nature, but perhaps only of marginal importance. With the many digressions, the theoretical discussions, the difficult interpretations of musical works, and the frequently pedantic tone, the pace is often rather slow. It only quickens toward the end. The last two hundred pages move fast and are gripping.

The novel consists of forty-seven chapters, headed by Roman numerals, and an epilogue. The first chapter is an introduction that anticipates important motifs and events in the manner of the prelude to an opera. Chapter XXXIV consists of three parts. Asterisks divide Chapters XXVI, XLVI, and the epilogue into two, and Chapter XXI into three parts. At the beginning of Chapters V, XXI, XXVI, XXXIII, XXXVI, XLI, XLIII, LVI, and at the beginning and the end of the epilogue, Zeitblom speaks about the raging war during which he is writing the biography "with trembling hands." These remarks on the war range in length from a few lines to six pages.

The number of chapters, forty-seven, corresponds perhaps to the year 1947, in which Mann finished his novel. The longest chapter is Chapter XXV, which contains the dialogue—or monologue—with the devil. It is forty-four pages long in the original and constitutes the center of the novel. By contrast, Chapters V and XVIII occupy only about five pages each. Chapter XXXIV, the second longest, has forty pages; it is important for portraying the parallelism between intellectual neo-barbarism and Adrian's *Apocalypse* and has the number of the magical square mentioned in the novel. Not quite accidentally, the lectures of Schleppfuβ, a devil figure, are described in Chapter XIII, a fact which pleases the narrator.

[70]

There are three planes of time in the novel. First, there is the time in which Zeitblom writes the book, from May 27, 1943[1] to about May or June, 1945. Secondly, there is the time occupied by the biography proper. In Chapter XXVI, Zeitblom speaks of the fascination which the "double time-reckoning" has for him; he distinguishes between the "personal" time, which is the time of the narrator, and the "objective" or "historic" time, which is that of the narrative. Thirdly, there is the old German past, the Middle Ages, the seventeenth and, above all, the sixteenth century. This ancient level of time is certainly unusual in the biography of a modern composer.

With its Gothic architecture, its neurotic atmosphere, its "characters," and its "witches," Kaisersaschern, which "never loses its hold" on Leverkühn, is a medieval city. Nepo, Adrian's charming nephew, uses medieval words and sayings. With his antiquated language, his table talks, his love of music, his vigor and sensuality, and particularly with his throwing things at the devil, Kumpf, one of Leverkühn's professors at Halle, is a caricature of Luther. Mann was fascinated by the personality of Luther, although his preference went to Erasmus. One of his last literary plans was a play on "Luther's Wedding." Kaisersaschern lies "in the heart of the Luther region."

Adrian himself uses the sixteenth-century language in the greater part of the letter that describes his experience in the brothel, in his speech before the people who have come to Pfeiffering to hear his last oratorio, and in his dialogue with the devil. His three major compositions are based on sixteenth-century works: *Love's Labor's Lost,* the *Apocalypse,* and the *Lamentation.* Many proper names have an archaic ring; they have been taken from letters and books of the sixteenth century, particularly Luther's letters: Sixtus Kridwiß, Zeitblom, Institoris, Ölhafen, Scheurl, Schneidewein, Spengler, Zink. Some characters, such as Adrian's parents and his uncle, are drawn after portraits by Dürer.

The sixteenth century is, of course, also the time of the first book on Doctor Faustus, the chapbook published in Frankfurt in 1587, whose plot is to some extent followed by the novel. Like Doctor Faustus, Adrian is a farmer's son, proud and brilliant; he is granted twenty-four years of an intensive life and is not allowed to love or marry anybody. He identifies himself with the Faustus of the chapbook, especially in the great scene where he takes leave of his "brothers and sisters" in the words of the chapbook; and Zeitblom agrees with this identification by giving his biography the title *Doctor Faustus.*

Ironically, or tragically, this third and ancient level of time is often fused with the first and second levels. The archaic, the primitive, the pre-humanistic, the anti-humanistic, was exploited and advocated by many intellectuals, artists, and political leaders of the twentieth century. This neo-barbarism spreads easily because, as Zeitblom knows—probably after reading Freud or Jung—the archaic layer survives in all of us (37-38).

In his lecture on "Germany and the Germans" (1945), Mann contends that the Faust of the legend and of literature should have been a musician, since music is a demonic realm. Mann's view and its fictional application in *Doctor Faustus* have amazed and perhaps also annoyed musicians as well as laymen who have been wont to see in music a source of sheer enjoyment, a gift from heaven rather than hell. But *Doctor Faustus* represents Mann's return to the atmosphere, thoughts, and emotions of around 1900, and in *Buddenbrooks* as well as in "Tristan," and later in *The Magic Mountain,* music is connected with decay, disease, danger, and death.

The superb analyses of musical compositions contained in former works are surpassed both in frequency and technical expertise by those in *Doctor Faustus,* to the extent that much remains inaccessible to the average reader. Outstanding are the interpretations of the last Beethoven piano sonata, opus 111, of the prelude to the third act of Wagner's *Meistersinger,* and of Leverkühn's two nonexistent oratorios. In addition, there are numerous references to the lives and works of Bach, Mozart, Beethoven, Brahms, Bruckner, Mahler, Hugo Wolf, Richard Strauss, and others, and a long discussion of a strange musical system invented by one Beißel. Though Zeitblom plays a musical instrument, the viola d'amore, it seems unlikely that he has the professional knowledge and the critical acumen that some of the analyses require.

While working on *Doctor Faustus,* Mann, who played the violin and the piano, read some two dozen books about music and musicians, enjoyed conversations with composers (Schönberg, Stravinsky, Křenek, Eisler, Toch) and other musicians (Bruno Walter, Otto Klemperer, Arthur Rubinstein), and had many talks with Theodor Adorno, a noted philosopher and an authority on the history and philosophy of music. Although he was bored by technical musical studies, he was convinced that one of the chief requirements of the book was a command of the musical technicalities, at least to the extent that no professional could scorn him (*Story*, 40). Although Leverkühn is a modern musician and, at the same time, a partial representation of Mann, Mann himself did not care much for Schönberg's twelve-tone scale—which Leverkühn employs—and for modern music in general. He preferred Beethoven, Schubert, Weber, Chopin, and Wagner.

Leverkühn stands for the artist who is burdened and inhibited by the heavy weight of tradition and technical knowledge, and for whom it is almost impossible to "break through" and create something new. Romantic emotionalism has to be discarded. Parody playing with old and lifeless forms is still possible, but not very satisfactory (241). The despair about impending sterility prepares the ground for a pact of the artist with the devil (*Story*, 64). To strip this statement of its legendary trappings, modern, bloodless intellectualism has to unite with bloody barbarism.

In his last work, the *Lamentation of Dr. Faustus*, Leverkühn succeeds in "breaking through" conventional forms and parody to self-expression, although, or rather because, everything in the oratorio is completely calculated and organized. While Goethe's Faust exclaims: "Feeling is everything," Adrian proclaims: "Organization is everything" (190). The expression of lament and final despair is apparently the only thing left for our late period. Mann's novel is, or at least wants to be, what it finally portrays: a "lamentation" and a "terminal" work. As a "terminal" novel, i. e., a novel which marks the end, the climax, and the limits of a cultural period, it has been compared to Joyce's *Ulysses*, Proust's *A la recherche du temps perdu*, Gide's *Les Faux-Monnayeurs*, and Broch's *Der Tod des Vergil*.[2]

Mann's old conflict between art and life, which seemed to have been solved or at least suspended a long time ago, is revived in *Doctor Faustus* and acquires a new significance. Adrian and Tonio Kröger are both outsiders and "inhuman," but Tonio thinks that love of the "human and commonplace, the blond and blue-eyed, the happy" makes a poet out of a literary man.

Leverkühn has none of Tonio's sentimental yearnings for the innocent and bourgeois. It is "love" of a prostitute, not of a bourgeois Inge Holm, which eventually makes him a genius. Rudi Schwerdtfeger has blond hair and steel-blue eyes like Hans Hansen, Tonio's boy friend. But Leverkühn has the mediocre Rudi, who made him happy and human for a short while, executed by a jealous woman.

Adrian belongs to the category of artists whom Tonio admires, but does not envy: the proud, cold beings who venture upon the paths of great, demonic beauty and despise mankind (*Stories,* 132). Adrian, too, thinks of bridging the gulf between art and mankind, but only bashfully, in a prophetic vision, and in general, not personal, terms (322).

The lonely Adrian calls love an "entirely exceptional phenomenon" since it means a conquest of previously existing resistances, based on the strangeness of 'I' and 'You'" (187). Contrary to Tonio Kröger, he does not long for any love or friendship; he is chaste, both physically and emotionally. His accidental visit to the bordello is a traumatic experience. One year after the prostitute had caressed his cheek with her bare arm, he takes a long trip to Pressburg, the present-day Bratislava, to meet her again; and although she warns him of her sick body, he insists upon "possession of this flesh." In Adrian's "fixation" and "choice" Zeitblom sees a "bond of love," but also "madness," a "reckless tempting of God, a deeply mysterious longing for demonic conception, for a deathly unchaining of chemical change in his nature" (154-155). The syphilis which Adrian contracts, and which he does not care to have properly treated, is indeed responsible for many painful or apathetic moments, for a rigidity in the gaze, and for some speech impediments, but also for extraordinary spurts of creative energy, for "feelings of triumph and power," and for releasing his musical genius. The Romantic idea of the "heightening" effect of disease, which is embodied in Castorp's development, reappears here.

The second meeting with the prostitute is equivalent to Adrian's signing of a pact with the devil. Whether one sees in this episode love, or self-sacrifice, or a loss of sexual inhibitions preparatory to a loss of artistic ones, Adrian's visit to the prostitute, whom he calls Hetaera Esmeralda—after the name of a butterfly whose picture he saw as a child in one of his father's science books—, is strange indeed, particularly since it involves Adrian's only heterosexual experience. This experience is hinted at in some of his compositions, since a five-note motif, a "basic figure of particularly nostalgic character" in a song and in the *Lamentation,* is composed of letters that suggest the words "hetaera esmeralda."

Adrian's homoerotic relationship is strange, too. When the violinist Rudi Schwerdtfeger, after months of wooing him, succeeds in breaking down the barriers of proud and cold isolation, Adrian apparently finds happiness in the warmth of human feelings (417, 437). But Leverkühn avenges this "humiliation" by sending the violinist on a mission which, as he knows, will eventually destroy the young man.

There are connections between Esmeralda and Rudi. Adrian meets the prostitute in what then was Hungary, and he apparently begins his affair with Rudi in Hungary. Zeitblom calls both, Adrian's letter about his first meeting with Esmeralda, and the one that initiated his relationship with Rudi, "documents" (144, 416). Esmeralda is an instrument of the devil, and in Rudi there is something demonic or devilish (351, 471). The promiscuous Hetaera poisons Adrian, and the flirtatious Rudi "wounds" him (416).

That Rudi has to pay with his life for his sincere feelings of admiration and friendship, is one of the enigmas of the novel. Mann himself calls the fateful last dialogue between Adrian and Rudi "an enigmatic affair with diabolic elements lurking in the background" (*Story,* 210). The episode of the assassination of a musician by a society lady in a street car actually occurred in Dresden some forty years before Mann wrote the novel. At that time, he had asked an acquaintance of his for numerous details of the story, which he planned to use.

Another, and completely innocent, victim of Adrian's love is his angelic nephew Nepo, who must die at the age of five because Adrian is not allowed to love anybody, or because of Adrian's "evil eye," or because of Mann's own self-sacrificial mood. Mann made his self-sacrifice even more painful, by having the "godchild" Nepo die of meningitis and by describing the terrible symptoms in great detail. It was one of the very few cases when he was moved to tears by what he was writing.

Doctor Faustus has been called a tragedy, or even Mann's only tragedy. Adrian Leverkühn, it seems, has to sacrifice human happiness, love, friendship, and his soul in order to overcome artistic sterility and create great and original music. His loneliness, his sufferings, and his madness constitute a heavy price. On the other hand, he is better off than many other composers. He has no financial worries,[3] can write what and how he wants to, and finally achieves the major artistic breakthrough he has hoped for. He is not handicapped by deafness, like Beethoven, and does not die young, like Mozart and Schubert. His living and working conditions are comfortable throughout. His genius is recognized by friends, publishers, and critics; and his works are performed by leading ensembles and conductors. If he had accepted the impresario Fitelberg's offer, he might have had the greatest social and professional success in Paris.

His end seems more pathetic than tragic, unless one believes that the devil actually takes his soul. It is true that Leverkühn identifies himself with the Doctor Faustus of the chapbook, and that at the end Zeitblom prays for his friend's "poor soul." But, in a way, Leverkühn has no soul to lose, since he lacks "that warm substance which mediates between the spirit and the flesh." In some respect, Adrian's self-identification with Andersen's sea-maid is more significant than that with the old magician. Like the mermaid, he is "inhuman," but sometimes and somehow wants to be human and to have a soul. In the very music, which is called soulless by some of Adrian's critics, Zeitblom discovers a "prayer for soul" (378).

Adrian's life and work are viewed as sacrificial by Mann and by the devil, though not by Adrian himself. Mann calls him a "martyr of his time,"[4] and the devil tells him: "You will lead the way . . . The lads who, thanks to your madness, will no longer need to be mad will swear by your name." Of these sick pioneers of humanity, Naphta says in *The Magic Mountain* that they die the true death on the Cross. By way of illustrating this point, Leverkühn's face becomes Christ-like; and even in his madness he has an Ecce-homo countenance (509).

And yet, to call the end of *Doctor Faustus* pathetic or tragic seems to be an understatement, for it involves almost total despair. Zeitblom sees Germany "clung round by demons, flinging from despair to despair," and asks: "When will she reach the bottom of the abyss? When, out of uttermost hopelessness— a miracle beyond the power of belief—will the light of hope dawn?" Zeitblom's lamentation is partly a variation and condensation of his own analysis of his friend's *Lamentation.* "At the end of this work of endless lamentation . . . the uttermost accents of mourning are reached, the final despair achieves a voice." The "dark tone poem permits up to the very end no consolation, appeasement, transfiguration." But the aesthetic paradox that expression is borne out of total construction may be paralleled by the religious paradox that "hope might germinate out of the sheerly irremediable. It would be but a hope beyond hopelessness, the transcendence of despair . . . the miracle that passes belief." In beautifully rhythmic prose, the miracle of hope is mystically explained: "What remains, as the work fades on the air, is the high G of a cello. Then nothing more: silence, and night. But that tone which vibrates in the silence, which is no longer there, to which only the spirit hearkens and which was the voice of mourning . . . changes its meaning, it abides as a light in the night" (491). In spite, or because, of that questionable "light of hope," *Doctor Faustus* has the darkest end of all of Mann's novels.

In Adrian's *Lamentation,* God's world and Christ are negated; but several other views of religion are to be found in the novel. Zeitblom pokes fun at liberal, rational theology, since true religion must be ecstatic and paradoxical (90), a view which is shared by the devil (243). Zeitblom also adopts Schleiermacher's conviction that religion implies the feeling and taste for the infinite (88). But he is truer to his humanist nature, as well as voicing Mann's own view, when he asserts that God is found in the respect of man for himself rather than in infinite numbers and an exploding universe; that religious feeling is only possible about man and through man, i.e., in the sphere of the earthly and human (273).

Zeitblom's Catholicism is not much in evidence. He never goes to church and does not refer to saints or the Holy Virgin. As for Adrian, even before his "pact" with the devil one never sees him go to church or pray. His anguish, however (shared by Zeitblom), about his not having a soul or losing it to the devil is great and sincere.

Different as *Joseph* and *Doctor Faustus* may be in world view, mood, and background, they have quite a few features in common. There is the similarity in the narrative technique, which is inspired by Laurence Sterne. Further, the protagonists

of both novels are men of genius. Young Joseph's pride lies at
the root of his brothers' hostility toward him, and Leverkühn's
pride is his deadly sin. Both radiate the atmosphere of "Touch
me not" (220), and both are basically chaste, though perhaps for
different reasons. Joseph is a prefiguration of Christ, while
Adrian, toward the end of his life, becomes a Christ figure of
sorts. Joseph stages the scene where he tells his brothers who he
really is, and Leverkühn, just before the onset of his insanity,
stages the scene in Pfeiffering where he tells the assembled
"brothers and sisters" who and what he really is. The lovely
Rachel has to die because of God's jealousy, and the angelic
Nepo because of the devil's jealousy (249).

The triangle Institoris, Ines, Rudi corresponds to the triangle
Peteprê, Mut, Joseph. Rudi refers to Joseph as his predecessor,
whom, however, he cannot imitate (349). Both Rudi and Joseph
please everybody. Institoris, like Peteprê, is not a real man; and
Ines is highly conservative and literate like Mut. Ines eventually
kills Rudi, and because of Mut Joseph is sent to the pit.

In both novels, the fluidity of boundaries and the unity of the
world are stressed. In *Doctor Faustus*, an all-embracing identity
of the most varied forms is mentioned (487). In the *Apocalypse*,
the crystalline chant of angels is identical with the howling of
hell. The boundaries between chamber music and orchestra,
between vocal and instrumental music are gone (457), while
those between health and sickness, between the inorganic and
the organic realm are fluid. Ever since his early years, Leverkühn has been speculating on the problem of unity, of interchangeability, especially of the identity of the horizontal and
the vertical writing in music (73). There also exists, at least for
Schleppfuß, the "dialectical unity of good and evil" (105).

As to some extent in *Joseph* and other works of Mann, the
fates and features of literary, historical, or contemporary figures
are used as models for characters in *Doctor Faustus;* but in the
demonic novel this technique of "montage" is used methodically
and excessively and does not even spare Mann's own family.
The actress Clarissa Rodde is a portrait of his sister Carla.
Clarissa's fate, and even her suicidal note, are identical with
Carla's. Mann transformed his second sister, Julia (who also
took her life), into Ines Rodde, who becomes a drug addict
and kills Rudi, her unfaithful lover. Mann's mother has be-

come Mrs. Rodde, the widow of a senator from Bremen, a rather superficial and frivolous lady, who, like Mann's mother, lives on Ramberg Street in Munich and retires to Pfeiffering (= Polling). The author later blamed himself for his "cold portrait" of his mother. Mann's favorite grandson Frido appears as Adrian's elf-like nephew Nepo. Rudi Schwerdtfeger has some traits of Paul Ehrenberg, a noted painter, who, like Rudi, was born in Dresden, played the violin, and whose undaunted friendship conquered Mann's melancholy isolation, as shown in Mann's letters to his brother Heinrich in 1901, in his letter to Ehrenberg of January 28, 1902, and in his "Sketch of my Life" written in 1930. Passages from these letters reappear in the description of the relationship between Rudi and Adrian.

The anglophile translator Schildknapp, with whom Adrian stays in Italy, corresponds to Hans Reisiger, a biographer, translator, and friend of Mann for many years. The originals of Schweigestill, Kridwiß, Breisacher, Unruhe, Vogler, Daniel zur Höhe, Scheurl, Kranich, and others are also known (Schweighardt, Preetorius, Goldberg, Dacqué, Nadler, Derleth, Kolb, Habich). The mysterious Madame de Tolna—a highly cultured lady who is very well informed about Adrian's works, life, and death, sends him an expensive ring, and is helpful in many ways (Adrian and Rudi spend some days on her estate), but who never lifts her veil—is modelled after Tschaikovsky's friend, Frau von Meck. Adrian's two other female supporters, the piano teacher Nackedey and the manufacturer Rosenstiel, are probably modelled after fans of Mann himself.

However, some contemporaries of Mann, especially musicians, appear in the novel under their true names: Walter, Klemperer, Ansermet, Monteux, Satie, Picasso, Cocteau, Joyce, Pound. No contemporary political leader, German or non-German, is named —not even Hitler, to whom Zeitblom so often alludes.

The technique of montage is also applied to Adrian and Zeitblom. They represent, among other things, two different sides of Thomas Mann. Neither of them is well described in his appearance. Of Zeitblom's face and figure we know nothing; he only has "a kind heart and a trembling hand" (*Story*, 89); of Adrian we only know his dark complexion, the color of his eyes (blue-grey-green), his "somewhat pointed chin, and his tranquil mouth" (21-22). According to Mann's *Story of a Novel*, this lack of information was intended to hide their true identities, but most readers find it inconsistent with the many details given about the appearance of minor figures. One entire page, for instance, is devoted to the face of Marie Godeau, the girl whom Adrian allegedly plans to marry.

Adrian shares some biographical details with Mann: He was born in Buchel—which is probably a kind of anagram for Lübeck —in June, five years after a first son; he does not carry on the profession of his ancestors, lives for a time in the company of another man in Rome's Via Torre Argentina—avoiding any contact with other Germans—and for two summers in Palestrina, then stays a short while in the Pension Gisela in Munich, and enjoys bicycling in the Bavarian countryside (204). Adrian also shares some artistic traits with Mann, for instance a tendency toward parody and quotation.

Above all, Adrian shows an extreme coldness toward other people, an "inhumanity," for which Mann has often blamed himself. Adrian has the greatest difficulty in using the familiar *du*. Only Serenus Zeitblom, whom he has known from his boyhood, and Rudi Schwerdtfeger are addressed in this manner. Zeitblom is never called by his first name. To mention just two examples from Mann's life: Ernst Bertram, a noted poet and critic, whom Mann had known for decades and who was his "best friend,"[5] was never addressed by his first name and never with *du;* and not until he had known Bruno Walter for thirty-four years, having been his neighbor much of the time, did Mann address the great conductor familiarly.

Mann loved Leverkühn more than any other of his creations, except perhaps Hanno Buddenbrook, probably because both incarnate some of his most intimate feelings. But since Leverkühn is, intentionally, a rather distorted portrait of Mann, and, in addition, a symbol of other things, his life, his opinions, and his works cannot simply be taken as representing those of Mann himself, even though the latter occasionally called *Doctor Faustus* an autobiography, or a résumé of his life.

Some events in Adrian's life can definitely be traced to Nietzsche. Although the latter's name is never mentioned, he is very much in evidence; the book has even been called a Nietzsche novel. His praise of vitality, his scorn of modern democratic civilization is influential in the Kridwiß circle. Adrian requests his friend Rudi to ask Marie Godeau to marry him. Nietzsche sent his friend Rée to Lou Andreas-Salomé with the same strange mission. Nietzsche's brilliance, his isolation, his "waves of euphoric inspiration" (*Story,* 151), and his death in madness are shared by Adrian. The insane Adrian is also taken home by his mother, and dies on the same day as Nietzsche (August 25) and at the same age (in his fifty-sixth year).

According to Deussen's memoirs, Nietzsche was accidentally taken by a porter to a brothel in Cologne, where he only struck a chord on the piano and then left. His insanity has often been diagnosed as a paralysis caused by syphilis. Mann, who believed in Deussen's unauthentic story, utilized it for Leverkühn and expanded it. Like Nietzsche, Adrian studies theology before taking other courses at the University of Leipzig. The name Leverkühn itself goes back to Nietzsche's preaching in *Zarathustra:* Live boldly! Even Adrian's diet in Pfeiffering follows that of Nietzsche. Zeitblom's moving last sentence, "God be merciful to your poor soul, my friend, my fatherland," is a variation of the sentence written by Langbehn at the death of his friend Nietzsche: "God be merciful to his poor soul." Some facts of Nietzsche's life, however, are ascribed by Mann to Zeitblom, Leverkühn's "other self," notably the study and professorship of classical philology and the military service in Naumburg.

The Jewish-French impresario Fitelberg finds that Leverkühn is a typical German composer, and that his production is becoming increasingly German (402). He mentions Leverkühn's discipline, his arrogance mixed with a sense of inferiority, his loneliness, and his refusal to join the rest of the world (406, 408). Similar to Castorp, whatever "typical German traits" Leverkühn may have, he is no German nationalist. He is even unmoved by the political and economical collapse of Germany after the First World War. With his shyness, his "life of a saint," and his brilliant mind he cannot be considered a representative of the new and brutal German nationalism. Because of its "decadence," his atonal music could not have been performed in the Third Reich.

The lack of a boundary between things and people in the *Apocalypse,* the rigid construction, the absence of a solo voice and of a free note in the *Lamentation* parallel dehumanization, regimentation, and mass culture; but these are not exclusively

German phenomena. Yet there is no doubt that Mann wanted Leverkühn to appear as a representative of Germany, a great German musician, imbued with the national tradition. Adrian reminds the reader of Schumann and Hugo Wolf, who, like Adrian, tried to drown themselves and both of whom ended insane. Adrian displays some qualities which were particularly visible and harmful in German National Socialism: a streak of cold brutality, a yearning for primitivism, and an icy contempt for the harmless citizen. Zeitblom sees in the *Apocalypse* a kinship with the drawing-room fascism and barbarism which are extolled in the discussions at Kridwiß's (353, 375). Curiously enough, those discussions, which champion violence, authority, "life," community, and primitivism at the expense of freedom, truth, justice, reason, and civilization, refer only to two French authorities, Tocqueville and Sorel; no German thinker is named. It would have been Nietzsche.

One of the reasons why Mann makes Leverkühn guilty of "automatically, coldly, and diabolically" causing the assassination of Rudi is to move him nearer to a system which was responsible for extermination camps. The madness in which he lives for ten years is also meant to correspond to the madness that gripped his nation for slightly more than a decade. It is perhaps significant that he goes mad in 1930, the year in which the Nazis won their first electoral triumph in the *Reichstag*.

Finally, Leverkühn is not only a symbol of Mann, Nietzsche, the German musician, Germany, and the modern artist, but he is, in Mann's own words, something more general, a "hero of our time"; he bears the suffering of the epoch (*Story*, 88).

Zeitblom, Leverkühn's biographer, is the incarnation of Mann's bourgeois, humanist, pedantic trends. He also shares Mann's political attitude during and after the First World War, his rejection of Nazism, and his uneasiness about an exploding universe. The little humanist Zeitblom also seems to share some traits with the great humanist Albert Schweitzer. While the professor and *Privatdozent* Zeitblom was born in the fictitious Kaisersaschern and marries Helene Ölhafen, the daughter of a colleague, the *Privatdozent* Schweitzer was born in Kaysersberg and married Helene Bresslau, the daughter of a history professor. Schweitzer, incidentally, was born in the same year as Thomas Mann. He, too, was a second child. Since he studied theology, music, philosophy, and medicine, he also resembles Leverkühn and the old Dr. Faustus.

By using a somewhat unworldly professor as his narrator, Mann tried to lighten up a somber story, and to relieve the impact of stark tragedy with humor. It "enabled him to escape the turbulence of everything direct, personal, and confessional." To "make the demonic strain pass through an undemonic medium, to entrust a harmless and simple soul with the recital of the story was in itself a comic idea" (*Story*, 31). Incidentally, it is significant that Zeitblom himself, like his humanist predecessor Settembrini, hardly ever laughs, while the demonic or tragic Leverkühn, like his predecessor Hanno Buddenbrook, often does.

Humor in *Doctor Faustus* is not only represented by the fact that the novel is told by a decidedly harmless, undemonic professor. The work contains a number of comic characters, incidents, and remarks. The translator Schildknapp, for instance, with his peculiarities and his stories about his father, perhaps the stuttering Kretzschmar, and particularly the verbose and quickwitted impresario Fitelberg are quite humorous.

As for the style of the novel, it is complex, rich and forceful. Again, as in the *Joseph* story, we encounter a great number of new compounds, nouns as well as adjectives. The most striking peculiarity of the novel is the use of archaic language. Many earthy phrases are taken from Luther's letters, the old Faust chapbook, or Grimmelshausen's *Simplizissimus* and form an effective contrast to the rather pale neologisms coined by the narrator or other characters of the novel.

As in Mann's other works, repetition is a dominant feature. Adrian Leverkühn re-enacts the destiny of Dr. Faustus. The farm of the Schweigestills at Pfeiffering is a copy of his family farm at Buchel. Both his father and Mr. Schweigestill suffer from headaches; they both smoke a pipe and die on the same day. His mother Elsbeth and Mrs. Else Schweigestill are both attractive, vigorous, understanding women with "smoothly drawn hair, just lightly silvered, with the parting in the middle showing the white skin" (326). Georg Leverkühn, the older son, corresponds to Gereon Schweigestill. In Pfeiffering there is a tree in the middle of the courtyard, with a bench around it, a pond, a hill, a stable maid, and a dog, all of which find their equivalents in Buchel. The "laughing" dog even receives the name of the dog in Buchel.

The three mother figures are very much alike: Mrs. Leverkühn in Buchel, Mrs. Manardi in Palestrina, and Mrs. Schweigestill in Pfeiffering. There are also three devil figures: *Privatdozent* Schleppfuß in Halle, the porter or pimp who steers Adrian to a brothel in Leipzig, and the devil himself, who in Palestrina assumes the appearances of the *Privatdozent,* the pimp and a music critic.

Repetition, of course, is also involved in the many quotations and parodies and in the technique of "montage." Quite a few quotations do not reveal their source, such as Shakespeare's plays, Hugo Wolf's letters, a history of music by Bekker, or the *Philosophie der neuen Musik* by Adorno.

Repetition is also evident in the pet expressions of many characters, such as Kridwiß, zur Höhe, Schwerdtfeger, in the descriptive leitmotifs, —Kranich's voice or Ines's mouth—, and in other, more subtle ones, such as the butterfly hetaera. Even more than in other works of Mann, the use of repetitions and leitmotifs appears at times artificial and constructed, probably intentionally so, since construction is an essential element of Adrian's music.

Doctor Faustus has been more severely criticized than any other major work by Mann. Objections have been raised to the almost complete reduction of theology to demonology, to the hopelessness of the end, to the condemnation of the whole German people, to the diabolical origin assigned to modern music, to the digressions, the many lectures, the difficulty of the esoteric musical interpretations, the interweaving of elusive personal secrets, and the paleness of the protagonist's personality. But the thoroughly German book is powerful in its very grief and despair. It contains a wealth of interesting thoughts, motives, and persons, psychological depth, and stylistic variety. Thus, it ranks very high among the many versions of the legend of Dr. Faustus.

CHAPTER 7

A Legendary Career: From Great Sinner to Great Pope

I N NOVEMBER, 1945, while working on Chapter XXI of
Doctor Faustus, Mann thought of stealing from his hero the
subject of the loveliest story which Leverkühn took from the
medieval *Gesta Romanorum*—the one dealing with the "extreme
sinfulness and extreme penitence" of Pope Gregory—and of making "a little archaic novel" out of it (*Story,* 147). In January,
1948, he began his customary perusal of sources, and in October,
1950, *The Holy Sinner* was finished. It was Mann's third legend,
after "The Transposed Heads" and "The Tables of the Law," and
the last work he finished in America. He needed something
comic after *Doctor Faustus* and enjoyed writing the "grotesque
legend,"[1] but he often said that *Doctor Faustus* was his truly
last work, that anything following it was a pastime.

His main source for the plot was *Gregorius vom Steine,* an
epic of 4,000 verses by Hartmann von Aue, written around 1200.
From Wolfram von Eschenbach's *Parzival* he borrowed proper
names, phrases, and details of courtly life, such as musical
instruments, furniture, jewelry, weapons, etc. Ferdinand Gre-
gorovius's *History of the City of Rome in the Middle Ages* furnished him with data for the description of medieval Rome.
In addition, he used the heroic *Song of the Nibelungs* for some
battle descriptions, Gottfried von Straßburg's *Tristan*—the protagonist Gregorius is also named Tristan—, Erich Auerbach's *Mime-
sis* (from which he borrowed Old French passages), books on
German life in the twelfth and thirteenth centuries, on German
cities in the Middle Ages, on medieval painting, and on the history of German literature. He also studied old paintings for the
portrayal of some of the characters.

Mann gives the medieval legend just as much color, atmosphere, and "precision," as he did with the Joseph story. Hartmann's epic, for instance, assigns no proper names, except to the protagonist. Mann wrongly assumed that his versions of the often-told stories of Joseph and Gregorius would be the last ones, that these respectful parodies represented the end of a cultural era, which was to be followed by a long night of barbarism.

In the night following the day on which their father Grimald, Duke of Flanders and Artois, passes away, the exotically beautiful and inseparable twins Wiligis and Sibylla, whose mother died in childbed seventeen years ago, have intercourse with each other. When Sibylla becomes pregnant, her lover-brother seeks to do penance by a crusade, but dies before reaching the harbor. When the child is seventeen days old, he is put into a cask together with some gold and a tablet on which his origin is written, but without the mention of any name. A bark with the cask bound to it is entrusted to the sea and lands at a Channel island. There an abbot baptizes the boy with his own name Gregorius and gives him a very good education. When at the age of seventeen Grigorß discovers his origin, he leaves the island as a knight-errant to meet and forgive his parents. After a trip of seventeen days, he lands at the shore of his mother's land, conquers her enemy, who seemed invincible, in a duel and marries Sibylla. When, after three years, they find out about their past, Sibylla does penance by working in a roadside asylum for the old, sick, and poor, while Grigorß has himself chained to a solitary rock in a large lake.

Seventeen years later, Grigorß is taken from the little island by two pious Romans and is elected Pope. Three years after his entrance into Rome, Sibylla, whose two daughters had helped her in her charitable work, has an audience with the "very great Pope," and fully confesses her sins. He absolves her, for "God accepts true repentance for all sins, and a human being . . . if his eye only for an hour grows wet with rue, then he is saved" (329). Sibylla becomes the abbess of a cloister in Rome.

Mann tries to dilute, rationalize or parody some of the suprarational elements of his source. The miracle of the bells of Rome ringing by themselves for three days to celebrate the coming of the new Pope is humorously attributed to the "spirit

of story-telling." In addition, the constant pealing is seen by
many Romans as a nuisance rather than a miracle. Mann "explains" Grigorβ's survival on the rock by the Old Greek legend
of Mother Earth's udders, which still secrete milk in a few
remote spots of the earth. He also has the penitent Grigorβ
shrink to a sort of prickly hedgehog or groundhog and makes
him sleep a great deal so that he can better withstand the in-
clemencies of the weather and the monotony.

About three hundred pages long, the novel consists of thirty-
one chapters, which have short titles, mostly of one or two
words, and a very short epilogue. In the first chapter ("Who
rings?") the narrator introduces himself. He is the Irish monk
Clemens, who writes the legend at the Benedictine cloister of
Sankt Gallen.

Much of the fun Mann had in retelling the old legend came
from his blending of different languages. His pretext was the
desire to create a supra-national medieval Occident which does
not know linguistic boundaries. Of course, the reader might
note that the monk Clemens should and would have written
his tale of sin and grace in Latin. But in addition to the prevailing High German and to Latin, Mann also uses Old French,
Middle High German, Low German, and English. A person—
even though uneducated—may speak several languages in one
short sentence. Some English words and phrases are used un-
altered ("dear me," "hoax"), others have German endings
("smoothlich," "Mockerei," "bosten," "swaggern," "Skrambel").
No doubt this is a continuation of the occasional linguistic med-
ley in *The Magic Mountain* and *Doctor Faustus,* but it is also
a parody of the anglicisms perpetrated by German immigrants
in the States. The linguistic mingling in *The Holy Sinner* has
been criticized as an unholy sin against the Holy Spirit of the
German language. Actually only a very small part of the novel
is affected by this mixture of languages, and the major reason
for it are its humorous implications. The legend also contains
some humorous plays on words, even some made by such rustic
figures as Flann (on "coward," "get ready") and his mother
(on "tramp").

Clemens rightly thinks that his style is "perfect and well struc-
tured." He also thinks that his prose, with its subtler rhythm,
is superior to verses and rhymes. Actually his prose, which is

often rhythmical and uses alliteration, sometimes changes into couplets, as in Sibylla's prayer (200) and, particularly and humorously, in the story of Grigorβ's first exploit, where Poitevin uses verses and rhymes against his own will (163 ff.).

The protagonist Grigorβ resembles many of Mann's artist figures. Because of his origin and sin he is "extra-human," he "does not belong to humanity" (144). As Adrian yearns to have a soul, Grigorβ sets out from the island to "win humanity" through pardon (145). He is an outsider in the "hut" as well as in the "cloister" (110), as Tonio Kröger is a stranger with the bourgeois as well as the artists. He is a brilliant student like Joseph and Leverkühn. Like Joseph, he is a living synthesis of beauty and spirit, nature and civilization. That synthesis, which in Joseph is considered extraordinary or even divine, arouses the hate of his foster brother Flann, who finds it to be out of the ordinary and confusing (123). Flann's attitude toward his refined and educated "brother" is reminiscent of the hostile attitude of Leah's uncouth sons toward Rachel's learned and handsome one.

Grigorβ is very successful in his first knightly exploit, although he has never been trained for it, as Joseph is a very good baker and Felix Krull a good tennis player despite a total lack of exercise. The three are potential players of many roles and potential carriers of many names. (Grigorβ is also named Credemi and Tristan.) They are beautiful to look upon, have dreams of future glory, and disdain a humdrum existence.

Grigorβ's success, for instance in his first fight with Flann, is based on the rare ability of "extraordinary concentration" (136). One may see here a symbol of Mann's power of concentration which enabled him, throughout many years, to write every day from nine to twelve regardless of the place and mood he was in. Grigorβ's "life" as a horny and prickly hedgehog is perhaps a humorous visualization of Mann's "pulling himself together beyond the average" (295).

When Grigorβ tells Sibylla that "every daring emprise on which he sets his all and uttermost springs only from the fervent yearning to justify his life" (192), he is paraphrasing Mann's repeated contention that his art is an effort toward salvation and justification. Grogorβ's hand, which, with its "extraordinary firm grip" (193-194), manages to drag a powerful adversary into a beleaguered city and thus to end the war, corresponds, in Mann's own words,[2] to his own tenacity in finishing his projects. One may particularly think of *The Magic Mountain, Joseph,* and *Doctor Faustus.* The "firm-holding hand" is a leitmotif of Mann's novel and his life. His extensive use of repetitions, leitmotifs, and correspondences is equally the work of a "firm-holding" hand.

That a life of "extraordinary concentration" outside of humanity may be crowned by the extraordinary position of a "very great Pope" may be seen as a parallel to the destiny of a "very great" artist who, in spite of his previous "inhumanity" may finally command the admiration of millions the world over.

As in *Joseph* and *Doctor Faustus,* pride is at the root of all conflict, evil, and misfortune. The incestuous relationship between Wiligis and Sibylla, their refusal to marry anyone, stems from their belief that "no one is worthy of them since they are wholly exceptional." They also have Joseph's conviction that "all the world must behave lovingly dévotement" to them (29). Wiligis later recognizes that pride was their sin, "that in all the world we would hear of no one else but just of us very special children" (46). After her brother's death, Sibylla keeps her pride, refusing to marry anyone except, seventeen years later, Grigorβ; for only him does she "find of equal birth" (202).

The "bad children's" pride is the same as that of the equally wealthy and handsome twins Siegmund and Sieglinde in Mann's "The Blood of the Walsungs" (1905), who commit incest at about the same age as Wiligis and Sibylla. The sexual relations between strangely beautiful identical twins who despise everybody else seems to have meant for Mann a symbolic twist of narcissism and thus closeness to the sphere of art. It is noteworthy that the protagonist of *Doctor Faustus* has sexual experiences only with a prostitute and with a man, and the protagonist of *The Holy Sinner* only with his mother.

The frequency of incest, and especially the first sexual encounter of the twins, has shocked some readers. In spite of certain details, however, that first night, when the owls screech and the faithful dog howls, is delicately handled, particularly Sibylla's blend of composure, curiosity, and desire. Its harshness is also softened by the use of an Old French dialogue between Adam and Eve. In the whole book, "only nature is indifferent or cynical," Mann asserted in 1952. He also approved the reaction of Clemens, who, in spite of all his indignation about the "bad children's" behavior, does not take the sexual sphere very seriously and thinks that the killing of the faithful dog is worse than the sexual abomination.[3]

The grave sin is based on proud choice and leads the sinner to being chosen by god. The German title of the novel, *Der Erwählte*, actually means "The Chosen One." There is hardly any doubt that Mann also thinks of artists like himself when he speaks of "chosen ones." Felix Krull, who is Mann's self-parody, significantly calls himself a "chosen one" (75). Grigorβ himself explains his being chosen to become a Pope by his very "inhumanity," which Mann so often attributes to the artist. "There was no place for me among mankind. If God's unfathomable mercy points me to the place above you all, then I will take it" (295).

At the end of *Doctor Faustus*, God's grace is only dimly seen as a "miracle beyond the power of belief." In *The Holy Sinner*, this miracle is shown to "choose" for the highest position in Christendom an extreme sinner who has undergone extreme penance. While Adrian Leverkühn ends in despair, Grigorβ knows before he begins his gruesome penance that man must not despair of God and the fullness of his grace, for God takes true contrition as an atonement for all sins (230).

In his last years, Mann often spoke of grace, and without any humorous overtones. He even said that his life and thought had been for a long time under the imprint of the idea of grace, and that it was grace that granted him the writing of the joyful *Holy Sinner* after the exhausting *Doctor Faustus*. He also insisted that, in spite of the travesty and playfulness, *The Holy Sinner* retains "the Christian idea of sin and grace" in all its purity and seriousness.[4] Yet it is difficult to see what grace means to somebody like Mann, who does not believe in a personal God.

Toward the end of the biblical tetralogy, Joseph invites God to the "play" of the recognition scene (1114). In the recognition scene at the end of *The Holy Sinner*, Gregorius "plays" with Sibylla and she with him—by not disclosing right away that they know each other—in order to "offer God an entertainment" (332). This levity is understandable in Joseph, who is a born actor, skillful and pleasing in many roles; but it seems inappropriate in a Pope, unusual though he may be, especially since his sin appears to be even greater than in the original legend.

While Hartmann's Gregorius sins out of ignorance, "to the blood" of Mann's protagonist "the identity of wife and mother was familiar long before he learned the truth and play-acted about it. In that place where the soul makes no pretense, he very well knew that it was his mother whom he loved." And Sibylla, too, deep down in her soul "where truth abides in quietness," had known his identity when she took him for husband, and only "pretended" at the "discovery" (328-330). This psychologizing or psychoanalyzing of the old legend corresponds to Mann's view of the basic identity of "happening" and "doing," "fate" and "character," but it makes the sin grow out of all proportions and also constitutes an aesthetic sin, because that "knowledge deep down in the soul" was never referred to before the recognition scene, and the shock of the sinners when they learned the identity of the marriage partner was sincere and not "play-acted." Mann lent perhaps too much of his playfulness to his characters.

The old legend is beautifully narrated. Alfred A. Knopf, Mann's American publisher, even thought that it was Mann's best-told novel. Mann himself liked it a great deal.[5] Whether it be the imaginary small Channel island of St. Dunstan with its fog and surf, the city of Bruges with its knights, elegant ladies, and burghers, the dilapidated Rome with its many churches and dignitaries, a dialogue or a fight, everything is vividly and sharply delineated. There are hardly any digressions or long descriptions. There is only one long monologue, that of the Abbot (84). Contrary to his procedure in *Joseph*, Mann rarely destroys the medieval atmosphere by anachronisms or references to the present. Among the few exceptions is perhaps the fact that soccer is played on St. Dunstan (116, missed in the translation). The story, which is so "extreme that the most astonishing thing in it astonishes no more" (327, 333), has shocked and delighted many readers. It is one of Mann's most humorous ones.

CHAPTER 8

A Portrait of the Artist as
a Young Swindler

WHEN Tonio Kröger, in Mann's famous story of 1903, re-visits his native town, he is almost arrested as a "Hoch-stapler," a swindler who passes himself off for more than he is. Strangely enough, the distinguished writer finds this, as it were, "quite in order" (119). For like a "Hochstapler," a writer of fiction pretends to have had experiences which he did not have, tries to create illusions by talking of things which do not exist, and wants to impress people.

Around 1909, after he had finished *Royal Highness*, Mann started writing the "Confessions" of the "Hochstapler Felix Krull," in part inspired by the memoirs of the Rumanian swindler Manolescu. Significantly, the family name of Mann's swindler sounds North German, his first name, however, points to Italy, which recalls the name of Mann's earlier self-portrait Tonio Kröger. Furthermore, the two family names alliterate. Krull also has the blond hair and the blue eyes of Northern Europe and the dark complexion of the South.

Mann was also fascinated by the idea of transposing the tone of the "aristocratic" confessions of his admired Goethe (*Dichtung und Wahrheit*) into the criminal sphere, thereby creating, at the same time, a parody of an artist's life and an artist's style. It was very difficult for him, however, stylistic virtuoso though he was, to maintain Krull's tone for any length of time; and so, in the spring of 1911, he interrupted work on *Krull* and started to write "Death in Venice," which, to most observers, would seem to be a much more exacting task. Krull's *Book of Childhood*, which is now Book One, was published in 1922 and aroused admiration. In 1937 Mann published Book One, subdivided into chapters, and the first five chapters of Book Two.

In 1943, after finishing *Joseph*, he thought of resuming work on *Krull*, "chiefly from the point of view of life's unity" (*Story*, 21). His wife and his friends often urged him to finish the book, but Mann decided in favor of *Doctor Faustus*. It is noteworthy that in 1911 he ceased working on the parody of the artist in favor of a tragic novella of a great artist, while in 1943 he set aside the comic parody in favor of a tragic novel of a great artist.

In February, 1951, while *The Holy Sinner* was being printed, Mann resumed writing the confessions of the unholy sinner Krull, even using the old manuscript. The book was published in 1954 as the "First Part of the Memoirs," that is to say, still as a fragment. It has about 430 pages; Book Three, with eleven chapters, is slightly larger than Book One, with nine chapters, and Book Two, also with nine chapters, put together.

Felix Krull writes his confessions when he is over forty years of age and has retired from a brilliant career of swindling people. He was born in a small town near Mainz. His father, a producer of cheap champagne, and his flirtatious mother often gave parties where "all restraint is abandoned." After his bankruptcy, the father commits suicide and the family moves to Frankfurt. His mother sets up a small boarding house, his sister Olympia, seven years older than Felix, embarks on a theatrical career, and Felix, who is eighteen, roams the streets.

Thanks to his godfather, the painter Schimmelpreester, he obtains a position as an elevator boy and later as a waiter in an elegant Parisian hotel. At a customs inspection he has stolen jewels from a wealthy lady, the writer Diane Philibert; and in the hotel, where she seduces him, she asks him to "steal" some more jewels from her. He has a sizable bank account and leads a double life. Because of his skill and charm he is professionally, as well as personally, a great success. One of the guests, the Marquis de Venosta, whom his parents in Luxemburg force to take a trip around the world so that he may forget his little girl friend, asks Armand, as Felix is called in Paris, to take this trip in his stead and in his name, and Felix agrees.

In Lisbon, his first stop, Felix is a great social success; he even has an audience with the king and gets a medal from him.

He makes love to Zouzou, the pretty daughter of the paleontologist Kuckuck, whose house he frequently visits, and wins the intimate favors of her "majestic" mother.

The parody of the artist has a philosophic or scientific background. As in *Joseph* and *Doctor Faustus,* the unity of the universe and the fluidity of boundaries are proclaimed. When he goes to Lisbon, Kuckuck tells Felix in the dining car that Nature constitutes a unitary system from the simplest inorganic element to life at its liveliest. The boundary line between life and the inanimate world is indistinct. Within the organic world, there are no clear-cut divisions between the animal and vegetable kingdoms; and the point at which man became man and was no longer an animal, or simply an animal, is hard to determine. Moreover, in the invisible atom matter took refuge in the immaterial (274-275). The universal and constant transcendence of boundaries forms a cosmic background and "excuse" for Krull's frequent and joyful transgressions of the boundaries of individual existence.

Kuckuck also tells his enraptured dining car companion that life on earth is only an ephemeral episode. Being itself is an interlude between Nothingness and Nothingness. It did not and will not always exist. Nothingness, absence of time and space, was only temporarily interrupted by spatio-temporal Being (271-272). Transitoriness, far from destroying value, lends all existence its worth, dignity, and charm. The whole of cosmic Being is given a soul by transitoriness, and the "only thing that is eternal, soulless, and therefore unworthy of sympathy, is that Nothingness out of which Being had been called forth to labor and to rejoice" (276-277).

Kuckuck's remarks echo Mann's, who expresses the same views in his short "Praise of Transitoriness" (1952). They are a radical departure from Schopenhauer's eulogy of Nothingness and from his own protracted fascination with timelessness.

Being, according to Kuckuck, is joy and labor, and all being, all matter partakes, if only in deepest sleep, in this feeling that disposes Man toward universal sympathy ("Allsympathie," 277). Krull, who is "extremely excited" by the scientist's talk about Being, Life, and Man, experiences a feeling that almost bursts the limits of his nature. This vast expansiveness, he feels, is closely related to, or rather identical with, what as a child he used to call "the Great Joy." The "Great Joy" seems to be another name for "universal sympathy" or "pan-eroticism," a term used by Mann in connection with his Krull. Krull's erotic desires are always directed toward the "whole" rather than a near and limited goal (48).

"Allsympathie" corresponds to, but is much broader than, Joseph's sympathy, which is the "deepest depth of his nature" (*Joseph*, 996). Joseph's "sympathy" extends to what is human; it stems from the fact that his "friendliness to life"—to human life, one might add—is balanced by "veneration for death." Kuckuck's "universal sympathy" is friendliness to the universe; it embraces the whole Being. Krull's "sympathy" (friendliness) is as "deep" as Joseph's. His charms and even his good looks, he feels, are only a manifestation of this "sympathy" (208).

Krull is, in the German title, a "Hochstapler," a name which implies that he pretends to have a higher social or economic status than he actually does, in order to impress and swindle the gullible. The name does not quite fit him because of his deep "universal sympathy." But there is a weightier reason why he is not an ordinary "Hochstapler." At one time he is an ill-housed, ill-fed and unpaid liftboy while, at the same time, possessing a sizable bank account. He enjoys this disguise and "deceit," this passing himself off for less to such an extent that subsequently he wonders whether he took greater delight in passing himself off for more (187). When he goes to Lisbon as a fake Marquis de Venosta, he feels quite satisfied, but not, he insists, because he is now an aristocrat; rather because of the "transformation and renewal of his worn-out self" (258). Krull is not so much a "Hochstapler" or "confidence man" as a born, artful, delighted, and delightful player of roles.

Ordinarily, roles, imposed by society, social situations, and professional needs, are rather rigid. When Krull goes to Paris, he recognizes that the train conductor is just the "marionette" of a conductor and he, Krull, only the marionette of a passenger. In their mutual dealings, their human backgrounds are immaterial. Krull finds this "unnatural and artificial" (119-120).

He rejects the rigidity of social roles. At one time, the "idea of interchangeability," an idea also dear to Leverkühn, haunts him in the Parisian hotel. "With a change of clothes and make-up, the servants might often just as well have been the masters and the masters might have played the waiter" (224). This silent game of "exchanging roles" is the "constant preoccupation of his leisure moments" (228).

He wants to be a player rather than a marionette. He does not like or accept the role imposed upon him by society or offered to him ready-made by another person. He wants to create roles out of his free "dream" or imagination. He, therefore, rejects Lord Kilmarnock's enticing offer, which ensures him a very good position and entails the promise of adoption (221).

This playing of roles mainly for its own sake is an artistic as well as an infantile trait. All his life Krull has been "a child and a dreamer" (48). As a child he used to play "emperor" and enjoyed the amused cooperation of some adults. In his boyhood he would wake up with the determination to be an eighteen-year-old prince named Karl and maintain this illusion for one or even several days. He did not need the help of adults then, but enjoyed the independence and self-sufficiency of his imagination. With charm and condescension, he conducted imaginary conversations with a governor or an adjutant of his (10).

The number of roles for which he is well suited is infinite. When he is a model for the painter Schimmelpreester, he can adapt himself to all periods, religions, and classes by means of costumes and wigs; any disguise looks natural on him. He is a born and enthusiastic actor, but only of those roles which he himself "writes." When he fools everybody, including the doctor, by playing "the role of a sick boy" (39), it is not so much the result of his performance that delights him—staying out of school—as the consciousness that he has creatively "corrected nature," made a dream come true (36).

His most successful, or at least most hilarious, performance is staged before the rather critical induction board, when, after a long and careful preparation, he manages to simulate an attack of epilepsy while appearing genuinely eager to join the army. Such feats require not only intelligence and imagination but also a high degree of courage and self-discipline. Indeed, his life is based on self-discipline as well as fantasy (51). He regards it as a "heavy and exacting task that has been assigned to him" (59). In this respect, and figuratively speaking, Krull asserts, his life has been soldierly, although for the sake of his freedom he had to avoid becoming a soldier (105).

Freedom means changing roles and names at will. As young Tonio Kröger "bore within himself the possibilities of a thousand ways of life" (98), Krull feels that he is "possessed of every possible potentiality" (146). Already as a boy, he is, therefore, tired of his name and disgusted by his ordinary clothing (47). The enactment of a theoretically infinite number of roles, based on imagination, concentration, and self-discipline, makes him a brother and comic symbol of the true artist and a living parody of Goethe's "Die and arise!"

Because of his urge or necessity to transcend the boundaries of individuality, Krull is fascinated by the "double image," in which the spectator—he is actually the only one in the novel to see this phenomenon—notes two individualities coalescing into one duality. Once, as a penniless loafer, he briefly observes—on the balcony of the "Frankfurter Hof"—a wealthy couple, brother and sister, perhaps twins. Their beauty lies for him in their "double" appearance, rather than in their individual appearances, and arouses in him "on many following nights dreams of love, of a longing for union, of primal indivisibility and indeterminateness, of a significant whole blessedly embracing what is beguilingly human in both sexes" (80-81). Later, in Lisbon, Zouzou and her mother Maria, before he even knows who they are, form another "double image," and stimulate again his "penchant for double enthusiasms, his fascination by the double-but-dissimilar" (287). To Mr. Kuckuck he admits that mother and daughter form the most enchanting double image on earth (308).

Krull's enchantment with the double being is a late addition to the novel and obviously a continuation of the fascination which the "double" exerts on Jacob and other figures in the *Joseph* tetralogy. In a way, and for a time, Krull himself forms a double being with the Marquis de Venosta, whom he impersonates. "We are one and the same," the marquis exclaims, "Armand de Kroullosta is our name" (252).

Felix plays his roles not only because he achieves self-expression (or self-suppression?) but because he loves people and wants their love. Although he has no useful occupation and thus apparently renders society no service—an important term in

Mann's œuvre—he is not like the "dilettante" in Mann's early novella, who is a total outsider in society, because he does not, and cannot, serve it at all. Krull's service is "Liebesdienst," the service of love. Even his serving of food is a personal service of love (206).

That he is "born for the service of love," as the prostitute Rosza tells him (114), is another fact that shows Krull's proximity to the artist or at least to some artists. After visiting the popular actor Müller-Rosé in his dressing room, Krull himself recognizes that love for the "yearning" crowd has made the actor a skilled artist. When this player of roles gives the people some joy in life and earns their applause, it is a mutual satisfaction, a "nuptial meeting of his and their desires" (30). Leverkühn had stated in *Doctor Faustus* that a "good artist means being a lover and beloved of the world" (132).

Krull's "universal sympathy," his "service of love," and the "nuptial exchange" between the artist and his public are connected with the fact that he also arouses homosexual feelings. During his beggar days in Frankfurt, wealthy men make him propositions. In the Hotel Saint James & Albany in Paris, the Scottish Lord Kilmarnock has fallen in love with him. Of course, his beauty, like young Joseph's, is literally startling; and even normal men, such as the director of the hotel in Paris, cannot escape his spell. Just as the "double image" enchants Felix, because to him it means original perfection, so bisexuality in the *Joseph* tetralogy was considered perfect, divine, and original. It should be noted that Mann's two great tragic artists, Aschenbach and Leverkühn, are bisexual, and that Tonio Kröger's and Castorp's "double images," Hans-Inge and Hippe-Chauchat, are bisexual as well.

While he excites men and women, Krull himself is sometimes enchanted by beings who seem to be neither men nor women: the "Artisten." While the word designates performers in a variety show or a circus, in the novel it is clearly meant to suggest artists. When Krull wonders whether the "Artisten" of the circus are human (190), when he calls them "world-renouncing monks of unreason" (191), one is reminded of Mann's gallery of "inhuman" artists who forego life and love. The star of the circus, the trapeze "artist" Andromache—a name suggested perhaps by the word "androgynous"—whom Krull "adores," is not human, neither man nor woman, but a chaste angel high above the crowds. What others give to love, Andromache's disciplined body gives to its adventurous art (193 f.). One recalls Tonio Kröger's rhetorical question: "Is the artist a man?", and Adrian's long years of chastity and loneliness in the disciplined pursuit of artistic achievement.

Because of his rejection of a fixed social role, Krull particularly enjoys the situation where he is simultaneously a poorly paid waiter and a well-dressed young man with a sizable bank account and a furnished apartment, who dines in expensive restaurants. "The charm of this dual existence lay in the ambiguity as to which figure was the real 'I' and which the masquerade" (230). Actually, he felt, he was disguised in either figure. In none of the "two roles" he was himself. This enjoyment of the two roles, neither of which he prefers, is perhaps representative of Mann's frequently observed delight in ambiguity and ambivalence, in seeing two sides and taking neither.

Like a true creative artist, Krull is a master of make-believe. One of the great experiences of his life, the memory of which makes his heart beat faster (31), is his first visit to the theater at the age of fourteen. It gives him "endless food for thought" (23). Müller-Rosé, who plays a handsome, graceful, elegant, and dazzling lady-killer, turns out to be ugly, covered with horrible pustules, and using foul language. This repulsive "worm" had deluded the spectators into believing that he incarnated their "secret dreams of beauty, grace, and perfection" (29). Young Krull recognizes that there is a "general human need to be deceived," and that people like Müller-Rosé (whose double name symbolizes his double existence) were created to satisfy this need. The art of illusion and charming deceit is "an indispensable device in life's economy." He also thinks that it is the drive of the actor's heart toward the crowd that impells him to learn the art of illusion, the same ineffable power that teaches the repellent worm to become a sparkling firefly at night (30).

As a child, Felix invents some games of make-believe which greatly entertain his family (9); and at the age of eight he practices the art of illusion before a delighted audience when he is given a small violin and a bow which is greased with vaseline and then "performs" a Hungarian dance in the music pavilion of the health resort. He also skillfully practices this art for his own delight, without intending to charm the audience, when, as a schoolboy, he pretends to be sick and when, later on, he fakes an attack of epilepsy before the induction board.

For his diversion in Paris he often goes to places where artful illusion is created: the panorama representing the Battle of Austerlitz, which is "so admirably executed that one could hardly perceive the division between what was only painted and the actual objects in the foreground"; a panopticon, where "you expect at every instant to hear (the figures) call you by name"; and a variety theater, where he watches a magician and a ventriloquist (163-164). As Krull's playful transgression of his self's boundaries is paralleled or pre-figured by Nature, so is his artful illusion, for Nature itself produces the illusory appearance of life in the inorganic, as in sulphur flowers or ice ferns.

For the same reason as Leverkühn, Krull regards love as an exceptional phenomenon in human nature, at least according to the lecture he gives Zouzou. He calls it the greatest miracle, which "annuls man's whole fastidious insistence upon separateness . . . wipes out the division between one person and another, between the 'I' and the 'you'" (361-362). Krull's long and articulate plea for love is in line with his innate tendency to transcend the boundaries of his individuality; but he makes it in order to overcome Zouzou's resistance to erotic transcendence, because she has the "childlike notion that love is the unappetizing vice of small boys" (358).

Krull, however, knows aspects of love which he does not care to show Zouzou. He had some first-hand experiences in venal "love" and has seen the sufferings and perversities of "true" love. The infatuated Eleanor Twentyman loses her common sense and endangers her future, and Lord Kilmarnock almost stops eating because of a "certain self-denial," as he admits to Krull. Krull thinks that he has never heard the phrase "self-denial." Actually, he did hear it, and some of its synonyms, from Diane Philibert. "Self-denial," "self-betrayal," "self-abnegation," and "self-degradation" intimate that even in love, when the boundaries of two individualities disappear, there may be the feeling of loss.

Diane, an incomparably more aggressive and articulate lover than Kilmarnock, also exemplifies another questionable aspect of love. A masochist, she demands and enjoys her "degradation" (173-174), as she asks Krull to insult and whip her. Humiliation is a state equally well known to Tonio Kröger and Adrian Lever-kühn, but not relished by them. Diane's meeting with Felix is, as she herself puts it—it is "her habit to put everything into words" (173)—the meeting of spirit and (stupid) life (or beauty). This meeting can at best only be short and illusive, as Mann has stated previously in "A Gleam." In "Death in Venice" and in *Doctor Faustus,* it ends in tragedy, whereas in *Felix Krull* it is a humorous episode. Diane, an author of psychological novels and passionate poems, fittingly represents "spirit" by being very articulate, using mythological and historical terms ("Hermes," "helot"), and making poetry during the very hour of intercourse. The handsome Felix fittingly represents life and beauty by experiencing the greatest sexual enjoyment and making Diane "very happy" (123).

In addition to being a masochist, Diane has a fixation on young men of about eighteen years. "Nothing in the whole world equals the enchantment of the youthful male." The "whole world of men and women and marriage is a matter of indifference" to her. Her love is "tragic, inadmissible, not practical, not for life, not for marriage" (177). Thus Diane's love comes close to being homoerotic, to the love of a Gustav Aschenbach for Tadzio, or a Leverkühn for Rudi. She herself calls it a perversion.

Diane is not only reminiscent of Tonio Kröger, Aschenbach, and Leverkühn, but also of Clavdia and Mut. Like Clavdia and Mut she is wealthy and older than her lover, who also comes from another country. Like Clavdia she has an indulgent husband, speaks French, and makes love once with a young man in a hotel. Like Mut she is very articulate, has an impotent husband, is the aggressive partner, and loves a beautiful "slave" (Felix is called "slave" by her).

In his old age, as shown in *Joseph, The Holy Sinner,* and the Diane episode of *Felix Krull,* Mann was much less inhibited or cautious in the presentation of sex than in his younger years. It is amazing that a septuagenarian succeeded in writing about sex with so much freshness, delicacy and vigor. In *Felix Krull* as in *The Holy Sinner,* he made it less offensive to some readers by using a foreign language.

Although Felix Krull is an artist in words, owes much of his successes to words, and is "exerting every conceivable effort to give" his autobiography "a belletristic form," he calls the word "a cool, prosaic device, a product of tame, mediocre civilization." Verbal communication is not his element; "it lies rather in the extreme silent regions of human intercourse," for only "at the two opposite poles of human contact, where there are no words yet or no more words, in the glance and in the embrace, is happiness really to be found.

This "supplementary observation," which Mann actually added to the earlier version of Chapter IV, Book Two, probably has to be understood as another symptom of Krull's interest and happiness in the transgression of the boundaries of his self. For "strangeness and lack of social relations maintain a free primordial condition where glances meet and marry irresponsibly," and "the greatest possible union and intimacy re-establish that wordless primordial condition." In that condition, there are "bridges across the chasm of strangeness that lies between man and man" (83).

This dim view of the word, of "manners and conventions," which define and limit, this love of the primordial, is partly responsible for the fact that Felix in his conversation with Mrs. Kuckuck, keeps using the prefix "Ur-," denoting the primordial, and that this prefix "steals into all his thoughts and words." In his eyes, Mrs. Kuckuck is a representative of the primordial Iberian race. Significantly, at the end of the book, a "whirlwind of primordial forces seizes him into the realm of ecstasy" with the same Mrs. Kuckuck and, contrary to the intellectual Diane, who was over-articulate in the same situation, Mrs. Kuckuck only exclaims "Holé! Heho! Ahé" before engaging in "the greatest possible intimacy." Incidentally, Krull's delight in the "primordial" realm of nature and his disparaging remarks about manners and social conventions recall Jean-Jacques Rousseau, another author of "Confessions."

Krull's "pan-eroticism" does not exclude himself and, therefore, leads to an unabashed narcissism, another of his "artistic" traits. He has a very high opinion of himself and repeatedly asserts that he is carved out of the finest wood. He is, by his own affirmation, priceless in his own eyes. This self-love, however, as he quickly adds, does not manifest itself in arrogance, but in charm, courtesy, and kindness (253).

Felix believes that he is a favorite of fortune and Heaven (9), who deserves his first name, Felix. He is a "Sunday child," handsome, intelligent, sensitive, imaginative, and "has the gift of good form" (290). It is particularly his "gift of responsiveness to the smallest and even the most commonplace pleasures" that has always made him consider his first name truly appropriate (285).

Like Joseph, he was born with many talents and skills. His mastery of languages is remarkable and before the hotel manager, he speaks three foreign languages, none of which he has studied. In Lisbon, he plays tennis reasonably well, although he has never learned it. The things he considers "innate in him can make one's head swirl," the maître d'hôtel tells him (201). The marquis judges by his appearance that he is a born horseman. He is, above all, a born player of roles, a born illusionist, and a born charmer.

All literary creations are, to some extent, autobiographies. This is certainly true of Mann's works, and Krull's autobiography can hardly be expected to constitute an exception. In addition to being the parody of the artist in general, Krull's memoirs contain specific data relating to Mann's life. Two entire passages have been literally copied from two of Mann's autobiographical sketches. Krull's "extraordinary gift and passion for sleep" (8) is also Mann's, according to "Sweet Sleep" (1909). Like Krull, young Mann was also conscious of the "independent and self-sufficient exercise of his imagination." One morning, for instance, he awoke resolved to be an eighteen-year old prince named Karl as he wrote long before *Krull* (1904 or earlier) in "Children's Games."

Like Mann, Krull was born on a Sunday, "a few years after the founding of the German Empire." He loves music (17), but dislikes school and does not finish it. After the bankruptcy of his firm, Krull's father commits suicide. In Mann's life the order is reversed. After his father's death, the firm, which had suffered losses, was liquidated. Both Mrs. Krull and Mrs. Mann leave town after their husbands' death. Krull's faking of epilepsy in order to escape the draft is matched by Mann's getting discharged from the army very quickly, thanks to the cooperation of a doctor.

Young Krull's vacation at Langenschwalbach near his native town, and his enjoyment of the music played at the pavilion there, go back to Mann's vacation paradise in Travemünde near

Lübeck. Incidentally, Krull's town is not named; neither is Lübeck in *Buddenbrooks* and "Tonio Kröger," though Travemünde is.

Twice Krull visits the Museum of Natural History in Lisbon. His scientific experiences there, as well as his feeling of "sympathy," are Mann's own. Mann twice visited the Museum of Natural History in Chicago and experienced a "strange sympathy."[1]

As in the case of Mann (and Leverkühn), his native town constantly remains in the back of Krull's mind (70). Like Mann (and Grigorβ), he "puts all the latent powers of body and soul" into any "great enterprise" (86). Like Mann, he also has a "talent for parody and gifts of burlesque travesty" (347). No wonder Mann, in the "Sketch of my Life," thought that *Krull* was, in a way, the most personal work he had ever written.

Paradoxically, Krull, who loves everybody and everything, who has a longing for the world and its people (8), cannot have friends (106). A brilliant conversationalist, he professes a bent toward shyness and withdrawal from the world (62-63). Although he can be "ecstatically filled with the spirit of a stranger" whom he personifies (146), the insistence on his privacy and reserve is a "fundamental condition of his life." His feeling that there is something special about him even "creates an atmosphere and emanation of coolness around him" (197). While his reserve may be explained as being the prudent attitude of a swindler, while his early loneliness is partly the result of the bad reputation of his family, and while that cool radiation is usually not in evidence, his loneliness is, above all, that of Mann himself and of his artist figures. His emanation of coolness is reminiscent of Hanno, Klaus Heinrich, and especially Adrian Leverkühn.

Thomas Mann and the critics have often called *Felix Krull* a picaresque novel in the tradition of *Simplicissimus*.[2] No doubt the novel has certain characteristics of that genre. Its protagonist is a rogue; it consists of numerous episodes; and it is told in the first person. But its general tone and its objective are quite different from the roguish novels of the sixteenth and seventeenth centuries. It is not a bitter social satire, and it lacks the harsh realism and the crude language. Felix is not a successor of Lazarillo, Guzmán de Alfarache, or Simplicissimus. He is not a simpleton who is repeatedly tricked and abused and has to learn the facts of life in a cruel way, but an enchanting master of his destiny and a master swindler. Dreaming of double images, leading a double life, being somebody else's double, he is, as it were, Duplex Duplicissimus rather than Simplex Simplicissimus. No good old-fashioned rogue would have rejected the advances of the wealthy men in Frankfurt, or the rich Eleanor Twentyman's passionate love, or Lord Kilmarnock's job offer and promise of adoption. No *pícaro* would have refused to use the word "whore" (174) or to repeat Müller-Rosé's vulgar expressions (27). The book almost reads like the parody of a picaresque novel.

To be sure, Felix, at one time or another, is a thief, a pimp, and an impersonator; but he is never shown hurting anybody. His juvenile thefts at the delicatessen store are insignificant. Diane is too wealthy to worry about the jewels which he stole at the customs office. He is courteous to everybody and has kind and understanding words for those whom he must disappoint, such as Eleanor and Kilmarnock. He does not commit his crimes, like a *pícaro,* in order to procure food or wealth, but in order to play a new and interesting role, to exchange the drab everyday life for a fairy tale or a dream (42), or to risk an adventure that would call upon all his talents (246). He "honestly" believes that he is an entertainer and illusionist by profession (197), and rebels against being labelled a criminal like ten thousand others (43). Not being that of an ordinary criminal, his life, he asserts, is devoid of "stage effects and rousing denouements, but rather appears strange and often dreamlike" (57).

Krull is not a *pícaro,* nor is he a Casanova or a Don Juan. He is not eager or compelled to conquer one woman after another. He gains the favors of the maid Genovefa, of the prostitute Rosza, of the author Diane, and of the housewife Maria Kuckuck, but they are the aggressive parts; they are also older and more experienced than he. When he tries to seduce Zouzou, he falls into her mother's arms instead. Although he thinks that "with him the satisfaction of love is twice as sweet and twice as penetrating as with the average man," he does not become a "lady-killer" (48). His difficult life makes great demands on his powers of concentration, and he has to be careful not to exhaust himself. The "crude act" demands an enormous sacrifice that leaves him exhausted and listless for a time (48).

Although Mann actually called *Felix Krull* a picaresque novel, the book was originally planned to be a parody of the most famous German autobiography, Goethe's *Dichtung und Wahrheit*. Goethe's "Fiction and Truth" was to be parodied as it were by Krull's "Illusion and Reality." It is perhaps for this reason that Krull is born near Frankfurt, that he spends some formative months in that city, and that he has one sister and no brothers. That the "First Part" of *Felix Krull* is subdivided into three "books," is probably meant to be parallel to *Dichtung und Wahrheit,* whose "parts" consist of "books."

There is a basic irony inherent in Krull's language. He reports the improprieties of his life in a style which studiously avoids any improprieties. To be sure, this polished language, which is that of a ladies' magazine, is one of the very reasons for his success as a swindler. The words are so smooth, pretty, and perfumed, as it were, that one almost overlooks their unsavory meaning.

No doubt, he is a greater verbal artist than his education or a purely realistic style would warrant. He skillfully handles a complicated sentence of fifteen lines, plays on words, invents one, uses obsolete words and forms (such as "Witib," "Marmelstein," and "größeste"), perhaps because he is "conservative by nature" (59), easily writes a difficult letter of twenty pages to his "parents" in Luxemburg, and without any preparation makes a literary speech of five pages on the subject of love, in which he uses some poetic words. He even indicates several times the beginning of a new paragraph. Incidentally, his double, the Marquis de Venosta, is also a greater player on words than most men of his kind and status. *Vide* his remarks on "wohlgeboren" and "hochwohlgeboren" (234) and the play on "heruntergerissen" and "Gerissenheit," which defy translation (249).

At times, Krull's style is over-refined or grandiloquent, for humorous purposes and in order to match the spuriousness of his existence: "The Rhine Valley brought me forth" (4), "I had blossomed into a most attractive young man" (63), "I must curb my pen" (84), the train ride proceeds on "wings of steam" (86), "I would not forgive my pen if it did not impart it some of the color" (189), and "my genitors" ("parents" on 340).

It is sometimes difficult to tell whether or not Krull speaks with tongue in cheek, or whether the reader should not be on his guard against placing too much confidence in a former confidence man's belletristic "confessions."

In September, 1954, Mann wrote that he would never finish *Felix Krull* but would rather like to write something more dignified and appropriate for his old age.[3] Yet the book was an instantaneous and unqualified success and sold more quickly than any previous book of his. Furthermore, the author of the *Krull* fragment had often scoffed at the artist's dignity, repeatedly affirming that his goal in life was to enrich other people's lives with cheerfulness, and that he was, above all, a humorist.

Actually, the book, originally planned as a parody of the artist's existence and of the classical autobiography, and later as a parody of the novel of education and of the picaresque novel, had developed into something which, in spite of all the amusing episodes, contains serious, scientific and philosophical thoughts. The comedy of artistic existence, however, carries its philosophic weight gracefully. In spite of differing elements and purposes, and in spite of the fact that Mann began it at the age of thirty-five and finished it when he was almost eighty, it shows a remarkable unity of tone. It is fresh, lively, very humorous, and a worthy counterpart of Mann's tragedies of artistic life.

CHAPTER 9

Stories

I *Introduction*

THOUGH Mann did not become famous until *Buddenbrooks* (1901), some of his earlier stories had appeared in important magazines and had been admired by qualified critics. Most of them are about a "marked" man, a person who is weak, sick, or odd, an outsider who cannot endure the triviality, coldness, or cruelty of everyday life. They are bitter caricatures of the young author, who felt like an outsider himself. "Little Herr Friedemann" (the "mann" in the name is perhaps not accidental) is born in June, like Mann himself and his subsequent self-portraits, Klaus Heinrich, Joseph, and Leverkühn. His first name, Johannes, is that of another self-portrait of Mann's, Hanno Buddenbrook. To some extent, the protagonists also symbolize the artist as such and his failure to live "normally" and happily.

Young Mann's psychological penetration is remarkable. The prevailing tone is one of cool objectivity or irony. The style is nervous and rapid; the sentences do not yet have the length and complexity found in the later works. Mann's famous leitmotif, the deliberate repetition of a word or a phrase for artistic purposes, is already in evidence, though still on a rather small scale. Examples are "lonely, unhappy, and a little queer" in "Disillusionment" and the "three chairs painted pink" in "The Wardrobe" (24, 27, 74, 76).

Some early stories are also held together by the same locality (the "Lerchenberg," for instance) or the same person (Mr. Schlievogt, Assessor Witzleben). Some persons seem to be sketches for *Buddenbrooks*. The towns, which are unnamed, are often hazy copies of Lübeck. The stories published after 1902 do not form such a homogeneous group. The lonely individual is still treated in some of them, but no longer as a queer and pitiable man.

At their publication, Mann assigned to individual stories, such as "Death in Venice" and "Disorder and Early Sorrow," as well as collections of stories, such as *Little Herr Friedemann, Tristan,* and *The Infant Prodigy,* the generic title *Novellen.* Few of these stories, however, seem to conform to traditional definitions of the German *Novelle.* According to Goethe, the *Novelle* tells an "unheard of event." According to others, it is supposed to be improbable, deal with just one event, have only unchanging characters, an extraordinary turning point, and a surprising conclusion. Among Mann's stories, "Little Herr Friedemann," "Little Lizzy," "Tristan," "Death in Venice," "Mario and the Magician," and "The Black Swan" perhaps come closest to meet these definitions. Most of the others are simply short or long stories, while some are sketches. In artistic perfection, "Tonio Kröger," "Tristan," "Death in Venice," and "Mario and the Magician" surpass the other stories. In the following pages, these four will be discussed first; the other stories then follow in chronological order.

II *Loves of an Outsider*

"Tonio Kröger" was first published in 1903 in the *Neue Deutsche Rundschau.* Mann had been slow in writing it; he had difficulties with the "essayistic center-piece."

At fourteen, Tonio Kröger passionately loves the handsome and popular Hans Hansen, who returns the feelings only moderately and, unlike Tonio, is more interested in books about horses than in Schiller's *Don Carlos.* At sixteen, Tonio falls in love with Ingeborg Holm, but only once attracts her attention—and that because of his clumsiness. His literary talent separates him from everybody. Shortly after his father's death, he contemptuously leaves his "narrow" home town and goes to live in the big cities of the "south." In Munich, thirteen years after his departure from his native town, he expounds to the Russian painter Lisaweta Iwanowna his ideas about art and confesses his love for ordinary life. While on a vacation trip to Denmark, he returns for one day to his hometown, where he is almost arrested as a criminal, and spends a delightful time at the Danish seashore. He sees two young people whom he identifies with Hans and Inge. His old feelings return, and he recognizes the two "chaste Nordic names" as meaning his "true and native way of love, of longing, and happiness."

The story consists of three parts. The first one begins in winter and ends in an "eternal spring" of creativity, the second takes place in spring, and the third in the fall of the same year. The first part is biographical; it extends from Tonio's fourteenth to about his eighteenth year, spent in his native town, and includes some general remarks on his subsequent life in the south. Most of this part is concerned with a walk and a dancing lesson. The second part is laid in Munich in Tonio's early thirties; but the author never explains when Tonio arrived there. What Mann called the lyrical-essayistic center piece is a rather nonlyrical essay in dialogue or monologue form. The third part is a description of Tonio's vacation trip to the north and ends with his letter to Lisaweta. There are no adventures, no plot, and no climax.

"Tonio Kröger" has neither the structure nor the content of a traditional novella. It is mainly concerned with the contrast between art and life, or rather between the artist and ordinary people. Some of Tonio's—that means Mann's—general assertions are contrary to widely held beliefs and open to argument. Art, according to Tonio, is not a profession but a curse. The artist feels that everybody sees in him a marked man. In order to represent human emotions effectively, one has to be extrahuman, un-human (103). As soon as one becomes a human being, one is finished as an artist. Warm and sincere feelings are useless; they only make dilettantes. The artist puts feelings on ice, analyzes them, and renders them calmly. Emotional impoverishment is a prerequisite for creative endeavor. Whenever Tonio's "heart lives" (which is not often), he cannot write well. For instance, when on his passage to Copenhagen the stormy sea arouses his old feelings for nature, his whole literary output consists of two verses, poorly rhymed at that. Tonio knows a novelist who has to escape into a coffeehouse from the atmosphere of spring and from the sensations which this most "dreadful" season awakens, because they prevent him from writing cleverly. One cannot "pluck a single leaf from the laurel tree of art without paying for it with his life." Whoever "lives" does not work. "One must die to life to be utterly a creator."

However, the somewhat self-pitying view that art is self-sacrifice rather than self-fulfillment has nothing to do with social criticism, i.e., with the artist's precarious situation in modern materialistic society.[1] Kröger does not attack society; he longs to be an integral part of it. He is a well-known and apparently well-paid writer and lecturer, and is invited to bourgeois parties. The conflict lies within himself. Not society but the bourgeois within himself causes Kröger's uneasiness, sadness, and bad conscience. His double nature springs from his origin. While his mother, of foreign blood, was sensuous and passionate, his father, the Nordic business man, was dignified, reflective, and puritanically correct. This origin corresponds to that of Thomas Mann's and is symbolized by Tonio Kröger's foreign-sounding first name, derived from his mother's family, and by his native last name.

His father's influence makes Tonio see another negative aspect in the artist's existence. Not only does the artist fail to live genuinely, but his work, so different from that of ordinary citizens, makes him suspect and disreputable. The repeated statement, "After all, we are not gypsies in a green carriage," only proves that deep down Tonio is convinced or afraid that he is a gypsy. And when, in returning to his hometown, he is suspected of being a wanted criminal, he is neither surprised nor indignant.

One can hardly subscribe to Tonio's two charges against the artist; that he does not live and that he is suspect. Quite a few non-artists lack warm, exciting, genuine lives, and quite a few are not always as harmless and sincere as Tonio sees them. Ironically, the exemplar in life for Hans Hansen, the idolized model student, ended as a drunk. On the other hand, many artists—including Mann—found true self-expression and a full life in creativity. Many artists—again including Mann—were also rather conventional and respectable in their private lives and even sensitive and constructive moralists.

Other contentions made by Tonio are equally questionable. While he writes to Lisaweta that it is his bourgeois conscience that makes him love the simple, the normal, and the respectable, one might just as well believe that it is the artist in him that is longing for the opposite and for relaxation. Indeed, Mann himself often spoke of the erotic relation between art (spirit) and life. Tonio's contention that only the bourgeois love of the human, the living, and the ordinary makes a true poet out of a mere writer, and that this love is the source of all "warmth, goodness, and humor" is completely unsubstantiated. When Tonio asserts that because of his double origin and double nature he stands between two worlds and is at home in neither, this is at least an exaggeration. One could just as well say that he enjoys life more than most people because he lives in two worlds. He is shown in situations, at a party, on a boat trip, during his stay in the resort, where the ordinary and harmless people do not see the marked man in him. And he has artist friends, even though he lives and dresses differently from many artists.

Because both Hans and Inge have blond hair, Tonio also thinks that the "race" of the blond and blue-eyed people stands for purity, serenity, life, charm, and happiness (108, 128, 130, 132). Of all the generalizations and simplifications in "Tonio Kröger," this is the most provocative. Tonio's racial theory or feeling seems to be naïve despite its Nietzschean overtones, and Mann never returned to it. Incidentaly and ironically, Inge's model in life had brown hair.

Tonio has been wrongly considered a lonely Romantic outsider in search of a friend and a home. It is true that Hans Hansen prefers other boys, that Inge does not care about him at all, and that he tells Lisaweta that he would be proud and happy to have a genuine human friend among non-literary people. But first of all, Lisaweta herself is a non-literary, though artistic, friend. And he also could have any number of friends among the intellectuals, the sensitive, and the "suffering." But for some reason, or, as he thinks, because of the bourgeois in him, he is only looking for the friendship of people who cannot or do not care to understand him, an unusual criterion for friendship.

Only in one period of his life—when he leaves his native town and soon afterwards—does Tonio not feel uneasy about the artistic condition. Art, then, seems to him the highest power on earth, towering above the "unconscious and inarticulate," i.e., the ordinary and harmless. When in the south he falls into "adventures of the flesh," he sometimes feels a "faint yearning of a certain joy that was of the soul" (99). This yearning, however, is still far from the love of life to which he returns years later. In the south, his "heart is dead and without love."

Tonio's literary production remains vague. As an adolescent, he writes some poems about the walnut tree, the fountain of his courtyard, and the sea, but then he writes something (novels?) full of humor and the knowledge of suffering. His artistry is fastidious, rejecting the pompous and the banal. It has psychological insight as well as philosophical depth. But no title, genre, plot, theme, or character is stated.

Much of "Tonio Kröger" is autobiographical. The native town is not named but, as in *Buddenbrooks*, recognizable as Lübeck. There is, for instance, a Holsten promenade and the Baltic (wrongly the translation has the North Sea, 87). The father is a respected grain merchant, the foreign-born mother plays musical instruments and leaves for the south after her husband's death. Tonio despises school and writes poems. His love of the sea is mystical. His love of Hans and Inge has parallels in Mann's life, too. He lives first in the south and then in Munich. His vacation trip to Denmark, some of the experiences during the trip, the public library in the old family home, the threat of arrest, the stay at the beach of Aalsgaard, all are taken from Mann's life.

Lisaweta Iwanowna has no model in life and has, therefore, remained colorless. She only gives Tonio tea and cues for his long and all-too-literary talk on literature. The "passionate and sinful" years in the south are not autobiographical either. This period constitutes the weakest, at least the vaguest part of the whole story. The "adventures" are not specified, no details about the "exhausting" life, nor a single day or incident are given. Mann led no "excessive" life in Italy prior to the publication of *Buddenbrooks*.

Some elements of the story had already been used in *Buddenbrooks;* for instance the parents, the walnut tree, the fountain, the mystical love of the sea, the decay of the family, the artistic way of life as a sign of the decay (98), the grandmother's prolonged agony, the river (Trave), the *Kurhaus* (in Travemünde) where little Tonio lives in the summer, the grocer Iwersen, the name Kröger, and the loneliness of the student. To some, Tonio looks like a more robust Hanno. Such a resumption of themes and names is quite common in Mann, especially in his early period. The dancing teacher and his name (Knaak) also occur in another story ("The Fight between Jappe and Do Escobar"); the homoerotic love of a fourteen-year old boy appears again in "Death in Venice" and in *The Magic Mountain.*

The style is often lyrical and rich in alliteration. Sometimes, as in the description of the raging sea, Mann uses onomatopoeia. Occasionally, however, we observe a certain verboseness and fuzziness. The use of the leitmotif, the literal or varied repetition of phrases and sentences, is even more pronounced than in *Buddenbrooks.* It is also felt to be more musical and is perhaps more justified, since the theme of return dominates the story. Tonio returns to his native town, he sees "Hans and Inge" again, is once more an outsider at a dance, and relives his old feelings. One of the symbols used in the story is the dance. The social dance means a simple, happy life. Tonio does the wrong thing and is excluded from it. He then has to dance alone the very difficult and dangerous sword dance of art (130).

"Tonio Kröger" is one of the most popular of Mann's stories. It has endeared itself, especially to young people, because of its adolescent melancholy and yearning, its often provocative statements about art, and its musical lyricism. One of its strongest assets is the impressionist yet tender description of nature, of a wintry day, of trees, of light, and especially of the sea. It was particularly dear to Mann himself. He counted it among his important works.

III *The Beardless Novelist and the Beautiful Pianist*

"Tristan," published in 1903, is a beautiful and lively novella about the deadly lure of beauty. Gabriele Klöterjahn, the young and lovely wife of a businessman and mother of a vigorous baby, suffers from a respiratory ailment and seeks cure in a sanitarium. There she meets a writer, Detlev Spinell, learns to see things from his aesthetic point of view, is induced by him to play Wagner's *Tristan* on the piano, and dies shortly after. The action begins in January and ends two months later.

The playing of *Tristan* is the climax of the novella, but its title also has parodistic overtones. Spinell, in a way, resembles the legendary lover, since he is an artist and has an affair of sorts with a married woman. However, he does not feel Tristan's passionate love and, instead of being united in death with his Isolde, only brings about, or at least accelerates, her death.

This parody of "Liebestod" is coupled with a satire on the artist, or rather the aesthete. Spinell feels at home only in the realm of beauty; he hates the useful, the practical, the ordinary—in short, "life." At the end, he symbolically runs away from life. He consciously overlooks reality and triviality or "corrects" it in his imagination. He does not really love Gabriele. To him, she is not so much a woman, a human being, as a thing of beauty, which he adores almost mystically from a distance.

When he sees something beautiful, he is beside himself and, contrary to his customary aloofness, embraces anybody who happens to be around. He lives in the sanitarium only because he needs the "austere simplicity" of its furniture for his "inward purification" (161). His only novel is printed on fancy paper in fancy type and deals with life in fashionable salons and luxurious boudoirs.

Spinell has not a "vestige of beard"; a cynic actually calls him a "decayed baby." He plays a pitiful role in his "dialogue" with Mr. Klöterjahn, who calls him a clown, a coward, an idiot, and a tramp; and he plays an even more pitiful role when the robustness and laughter of a baby puts him to flight. Although he is the main figure of the novella, he is referred to three times merely as "a writer" before the author gives his name and speaks of him as "the writer." Mann obviously treats him with unmitigated irony, which, in a way, is directed against himself. Together with Tonio Kröger, Gustav Aschenbach, and Adrian Leverkühn, Spinell belongs to the line of Mann's lonely artists. He is the only ridiculous and the least talented one.

But there is something sinister in this ridiculous and ridiculed writer. He urges Mrs. Klöterjahn to play music, although it endangers her health, as he well knows. When he hears about her impending death, he has no pangs of conscience, feels no sympathy, does not even seem to think of her, looks at himself in the mirror—which is symbolic of the artist's self-centeredness—drinks some cognac, and is only annoyed about Mr. Klöterjahn's misuse of words. Although he witnesses the death of a lovely young person and sees the grief and sorrow of two other persons, he calls the whole experience "crude." His lack of human sensitivity is almost incredible. He completely lacks the "good, warm, honest human feeling" shown by Mr. Klöterjahn, whom he despises as a "greedy plebeian."

His letter to Klöterjahn shows the comic as well as the sinister side of his existence. It is ridiculous because Klöterjahn is right in the sanitarium and because it is full of bombast and conceit. But he also insults the husband of a gravely sick woman, who has done him no harm, tells him that he hates him as well as his child, and that his wife is happy and proud to die from the kiss of beauty.

The novella clearly shows the antitheses which are characteristic of the early Mann. On one side there is health, life, activity, normality, warmth, simplicity, business, usefulness, individuality, sunshine; on the other side there is sickness, death, beauty, dream, spirit, literature, sophistication, music, self-obliteration, and night. Since Mrs. Klöterjahn is forbidden to play the piano for reasons of health, the music from *Tristan,* exalting the charms of night, death, and eternity, is the worst possible one for her to select. It is characteristic not only of Mann's musical taste but also of the antithesis night-day that she plays three Chopin nocturnes before *Tristan.*

The style is generally ironic and marked by the use of leit-motifs. The most obvious of these is the strange little vein that arches pale-blue and sickly across Mrs. Klöterjahn's brow. The most curious one, unfortunately lost in the translation, is the seemingly innocuous "übrigens" (by the way), that thrice introduces a sentence stating which of the two doctors is in charge.

There is a complete change in atmosphere and a break in style when Mrs. Klöterjahn plays *Tristan.* Mann has always been a master in knowingly analyzing, as well as poetically suggesting, music. The style becomes rhythmical, exalted, and contains exclamations, apostrophes ("O night of love!"), alliteration, onomatopoeia, rhymes, questions, repetitions, and metaphors. But even this ecstatic climax is used to produce ironic effects. Mrs. Spatz leaves the room because the beautiful music is a deadly bore to her; and the insane Mrs. Höhlenrauch interrupts the music by walking through the room "rigid and still."

The novella reminds the reader of *Buddenbrooks,* especially in the antitheses. Klöterjahn is also a business man from

Lübeck, though, as in *Buddenbrooks* and "Tonio Kröger," the city is not named. Like Gerda Buddenbrook, Gabriele is the daughter of a merchant who plays the violin, and she herself is highly musical. *Buddenbrooks* as well as "Tristan" tell of a wintry day with its billions of atoms of light, of a nursemaid in red and gold, and of the transfiguration of an old and decaying bourgeois family through music. The novella shares with "Death in Venice" the connection between beauty and death, with *The Magic Mountain* the sanitarium in the mountains, the authoritarian chief doctor, and the fascination with death, and with *Doctor Faustus* the inhuman artist who is responsible for the death of an angelic person, the importance of music, and the parodistic title.

IV   Beauty and the Abyss

"Death in Venice" ("Der Tod in Venedig") was first published in 1912 as a "Novelle" in two installments. Mann had interrupted his work on the humorous *Felix Krull* to write this tragic story.

Gustav Aschenbach, a greatly admired writer over fifty years of age, notices an exotic-looking man at the edge of a Munich cemetery and, out of a sudden yearning for distant scenes, goes to an Adriatic island, but, being disappointed, he leaves after ten days for Venice, where a strange gondolier takes him to the Lido. At the hotel, he sees Tadzio, a Polish boy of fourteen, whose "perfect, almost godlike" beauty he first admires with the "cool approval of a connoisseur" only. Because of an unpleasant wind, the constant sultriness and a foul smell, he decides to leave for a resort near Trieste. But when he learns at the station that his trunk was sent to a wrong place, he returns to the hotel and decides to stay there. He now enjoys the sea and the sun and falls madly in love with Tadzio. Although he later finds out that there is a cholera epidemic in Venice, which the authorities conceal from the public, he does not leave. No longer hiding his passion for the boy, he often follows him through the streets. On the day when Tadzio's family is scheduled to leave Venice, the writer dies on the beach.

Like little Hanno Buddenbrook, the early Thomas Mann was fascinated by death. For years he held the awe of death as a foundation of religious feeling. Not until the *Magic Mountain* was he somehow liberated from this spell and enrolled in the "service of life." Acording to the novella, that fascination with death, destruction, and chaos, with the "abyss," is inherent in art. "Knowledge," i.e., depth psychology, "has compassion with the abyss—it is the abyss" (435). The artist, with Aschenbach, may reject this "knowledge" and be concerned solely with beauty, i.e., form. But there is no escape from the abyss. For "detachment and preoccupation with form lead to intoxication and desire . . . to frightful emotional excesses . . . So, they, too, lead to the bottomless pit." This is Aschenbach's philosophic conclusion a few days before his death. It shares with Plato not only the form (of a philosophical dialogue or rather monologue), but also the deep distrust of the artist.

To be sure, Aschenbach's final philosophical sentences are said to be "shaped in a disordered brain by the fantastic logic that governs our dreams" (434) and, therefore, may not be readily identified with Thomas Mann. But at the beginning of the story, the narrator himself, expressing similar ideas, shows what happens when an artist "renounces sympathy with the abyss" (386). While form is moral in so far as it is the expression and result of discipline, it is immoral since it is indifferent to good and evil. About ten years after the publication of "Death in Venice," Mann still maintained in a letter to Count Keyserling "On Marriage" that "the artist inclines toward the abyss."

Aschenbach's encounter with Tadzio signifies the encounter of intellect with beauty, or spirit with life, an encounter which, according to Mann's views, is bound to be short, unsatisfactory, and fruitless. Tonio Kröger and Hans Hansen enact a slightly melancholy, Adrian Leverkühn and Rudi Schwerdtfeger a tragic, Diane Philibert and Felix Krull a parodistic version of this encounter. In "Death in Venice," spirit and beauty have confusing and perhaps conflicting claims, although Aschenbach's personal relationship with Tadzio seems to be unambiguous. Aschenbach offers himself up in spirit to create beauty while Tadzio is a possessor of beauty (403). This seems to imply an identification of spirit and art. According to Aschenbach-Socrates' early lecture to Phaedrus, beauty is but an aspect of the spiritual (413). But in his last imaginary lecture, art seems to be separated from spirit, and beauty seems only an intermediary between the two: Beauty is the artist's way to the spirit (434). While this statement may be ascribed to Aschenbach's "dream logic," it must be said that Mann's own views on the relationship between art, life (often identified with beauty or symbolized by beauty), and spirit are rather confusing. In the course of his life, these three concepts seem to have played the game of musical chairs. Sometimes two of them sit on the same chair. Art, for instance, is at times the intermediary between life and spirit, sometimes identical with spirit, sometimes with life ("Art is heightened life," 388), sometimes eternally opposed to life.

Another relationship confusing to most readers of Mann is that between love and life. Biologically, love springs from life and leads to life; emotionally, it often is life at its liveliest and best. When Tonio Kröger feels love, his heart lives; usually it does not. Yet in German Romanticism, in a great part of Mann's *Magic Mountain,* and in "Death in Venice," love is tied up with disease and death. There are several reasons for this "perversion." First, both love and death shatter the frontiers of the individual. Second, Aschenbach's love for Tadzio, like Diane's love for Krull or Castorp's love for Clavdia, is "nothing for life," as Diane says; it has nothing to do with children and marriage.

Third and most important, Aschenbach's death is that combination of love and death which is so dear to some German Romantics and celebrated particularly in Wagner's *Tristan:* the "Liebestod." Mann liked to play the "Liebestod" on the piano. Hanno improvises on the piano the "Liebestod" on the level of weakness and masturbation; Mrs. Klöterjahn plays the "Liebestod" from *Tristan* on the level of disease and platonic curiosity, while Mrs. Tümmler in "The Black Swan" experiences it on a level of disease and delusion and Aschenbach "lives" it on the level of disease and homoeroticism. In Aschenbach's dream of a wild orgy of promiscuous embraces, love, or rather sex, is connected with disease; there is the "odor of wounds, uncleanliness, and disease" (431). In his French speech to Clavdia Chauchat in the *Magic Mountain,* Hans Castorp proclaims the unity of disease, love, and death. Thus, "Liebestod" seems to have a definite pathological twist in Mann's works.

Still another relationship which is perplexing to many readers is that between the sea and death. In a speech celebrating Gerhart Hauptmann's sixtieth birthday, Mann asserted that love of the sea is nothing but love of death. And in his speech on "Lü-beck as a Spiritual Way of Life," he calls the sea the experience of nothingness and death. One of the "profound sources" of Aschenbach's love of the sea is his "yearning for the unorganized, for nothingness" (401). His urge to go to a sea resort may, therefore, be taken as a symptom of his never completely suppressed yearning for chaos and death. Incidentally, Thomas Mann, Thomas and Hanno Buddenbrook, Tonio Kröger, Hans Castorp, and Gustav Aschenbach love a land-locked sea—the Baltic, the North Sea, or the Adriatic—not an Ocean. Thomas Mann once said that neither the Atlantic nor the Pacific aroused him as much as a land-locked sea.[2]

The novella or, as some prefer to call it, the small novel is written with consummate skill. There are no extraneous or accidental elements. Words, sentences, and persons often have several meanings, can be interpreted on several levels, and are interconnected in many ways. Mann himself asserted, probably with some exaggeration, that nothing had been invented in "Death in Venice," but he also maintained that even insignificant details are symbolical and that the story has many facets.

Aschenbach himself, for instance, is first the artist per se, whose downfall and death exemplify the impossibility of an artist's ever achieving perfect beauty and dignity. He is also the special type of artist who forgets that art demands dissoluteness as well as discipline, who exerts rigid and cold discipline in the cult of form, and who, therefore, succumbs to frantic dissolution, as if life (or death) were cruelly taking revenge for being neglected. He is also, like Mann, a specific human type, that of the "moralizer of achievement," whose accomplishments are made in spite of all the internal and external obstacles, "in defiance of affliction and pain, poverty, destitution, bodily weakness, vice, passion, and a thousand other obstructions" (384). He, therefore, is the poet-spokesman of all those who labor on the brink of exhaustion.

Aschenbach is also Thomas Mann. Like his author, he resides in Munich—even in the same neighborhood—has a summer home in the Bavarian Alps, has the habit of working in the morning and sleeping in the afternoon, is married to a scholar's daughter, loves the sea and Venice. He has treated similar themes and figures; one recognizes allusions to *Buddenbrooks,* "Tonio

Kröger," the play *Fiorenza,* and *Felix Krull.* Just like Thomas Mann in 1911, he leaves Munich in May for an Istrian island, after ten days departs from that resort because it does not agree with him, goes to Venice, and stays in the Hôtel des Bains. He suggests also the composer Gustav Mahler, whose external appearance and first name he borrows. He also reminds one, as one critic suggested, of the German poet Platen, or, as another thought, of Richard Wagner, who actually died in Venice.[3]

Tadzio, the handsome but fragile Polish boy of fourteen, means many things, too. He represents perfect beauty, the tantalizing and unattainable goal of a classical writer, or again the projection of the narcissistic tendencies inherent in the artist. He is the boy-god Eros as well as Hermes, Thomas Mann's favorite Greek god, who, among many other things, leads the souls to the realm of death. At the end of the novella, Tadzio is called a *Psychagog,* a leader of souls. It is perhaps not accidental that three of the six letters in his name form the German word for death: *Tod.*

The man carrying the rucksack at the edge of the cemetery, the weird gondolier, and the street singer are, at first sight, different individuals and have different jobs. According to his short autobiography, Mann had actually seen them before or during one of his stays in Venice. But the three have a strange resemblance. With some allowance made for slight deviations, they are of medium height or undersized, thin, beardless, snub-nosed, red-haired, foreign looking; they wear something yellow, have two furrows on their forehead, bare their teeth, and have a strikingly large Adam's apple. They look bold, provocative, or even dangerous. The man whom Aschenbach sees at the cemetery, the man who handles the gondola, a conveyance "black as nothing else on earth except a coffin" (392), and the singer with the strong smell of carbolic acid all suggest the traditional pictorial representation of death.

The three men do not belong to the place where they are seen. They are strangers. The man at the Munich cemetery is not from Munich, the gondolier and the singer are not Venetians. This fact is connected with Aschenbach's emotions. The man at the cemetery makes Aschenbach long for foreign countries. Aschenbach adores a foreign boy, experiences feelings which have been foreign to him, and his wild dream culminates in the homage to the "stranger god." This god, Dionysos, incidentally has some connections with India, from which the cholera came. The three men not only suggest the spell of that which is foreign but also lawlessness and chaos; the man at the cemetery has no visible aim, the gondolier has no "concession," and the singer laughs "as if possessed."

No wonder that the three have also been viewed as projections of Aschenbach's repressed yearning for death or his secret craving for the strange, the forbidden or the chaotic. It is perhaps not accidental that Aschenbach resembles the three strangers. He is below middle height, beardless, bold ("heroic"), and a stranger: He was not born in Munich where he resides, is repeatedly called a stranger or a foreigner (419, 427, 429), and his appearance shows "foreign traits" (382). Nor is it perhaps accidental that his name begins with Aschen (ashes), a symbol of death.

The choice of Venice as the locale of the novella is related to different reasons. Venice was a favorite resort of Thomas Mann. It reminded him in many ways of his native Lübeck. The background of Venice fits Aschenbach's personality and death: The city has been an inspiration to artists, painters as well as musicians (421); and it also is a dying city which has lost much of its ancient grandeur. Further, it is the city where Wagner died. In an essay on the composer, Mann called it the city of *Tristan*, and *Tristan* means for Mann mainly the "Liebestod." Venice is also the locale of "Disillusionment," one of Mann's earliest stories (1896). Like "Death in Venice," "Disillusionment" is, to some extent, a censure of literature.

The novella offers more or less overt connections, double and triple meanings, parallels, and identifications. The title itself is equivocal. It may refer to the death caused to many by the cholera, or solely to Aschenbach's death, or to both.

In spite of the many meanings, connections, and interpretations, and in spite of the richness of the vocabulary and the wealth of images, the style seems firm and direct. And in spite of the frenzied emotions and the terrible plague, the narration is controlled and objective. It is ironical or paradoxical that a story purported to show how low the artist can and must sink, is told with the most elevated art.

The narration proceeds in a straight line. There are only two flashbacks. One relates Aschenbach's past, the other the history of the cholera. It is May when Aschenbach has the vision of a lush, "tropical marshland, beneath a reeking sky, streaming, monstrous, rank . . . where the water was stagnant and the eyes of a crouching tiger gleamed," a vision which eventually takes him to Venice and to his death. And it is May when the cholera, originating in the hot, moist swamps of the delta of the Ganges, "where it bred in the mephitic air of that primeval island-jungle, among whose bamboo thickets the tiger crouches" (427), comes to Venice and spreads death there. There is also a connection, sometimes even to the point of identification, between the secrecy surrounding the plague in the beginning, the ensuing danger, the breakdown of morality on one side and Aschenbach's passion, which he first tries to keep secret and which brings about a collapse of his morality, on the other.

The names used in "Death in Venice" are mostly those of well-known persons of the past, such as Socrates, Phaedrus, Cicero, Saint Sebastian, Louis XIV, Frederick the Great, Voltaire, or of Greek mythological figures, such as Zeus, Semele, Eros, Narcissus, Hyacinthus, Poseidon. This is an outward manifestation of the story's stress on the mythical, the foreign, greatness, and death.

The mythology of "Death in Venice" is mainly based on the *Odyssey* and on Erwin Rohde's *Psyche*, one of the most influential books on Greek religion. In *Psyche* reference is made to the Dionysian frenzy in Euripides' *Bacchae*.[4] *Bacchae* may have influenced Aschenbach's dream of the orgy and the "stranger God." In Euripides' play, Dionysus comes from Asia and is called a foreigner. The main theme of *Bacchae* is also an important one in "Death in Venice": When a person fights against passions and denies them instead of recognizing them as the essence of life, they will become ugly and destroy him.[5]

The use of Greek mythology, of a hexameter by Homer, of dactylic rhythm, internal Platonic dialogues or monologues in an otherwise realistic story of a twentieth-century writer may seem peculiar. There probably are three main reasons for it. First, Aschenbach, whose style shows an "almost exaggerated sense of beauty, a lofty purity, symmetry, and simplicity" and has a "stamp of the classic" (386), is a classical writer and, therefore, may be connected with classical antiquity. Second, the use of ancient Greek cultural elements widens and deepens the story and perhaps raises its conflict to a mythical level. And third, the allusions to antiquity and its different moral and religious standards definitely softened the blow that many readers felt at the time of the publication of the novella because of the theme of homosexuality. Few modern writers before Mann dared to deal with such a topic. Mann was greatly interested in homosexuality. There is an allusion of several lines to Platen (391). Platen, a nineteenth-century German lyricist, who, like Aschenbach, revered beautiful form, who, again like Aschenbach, was in love with Venice, and whose homoerotic interests are well known thanks to Heinrich Heine, wrote a poem—repeatedly quoted by Mann, although not in "Death in Venice"—whose first two lines might be a motto of the novella: "He whose eyes have looked at beauty is a prey of death already."

The aging Thomas Buddenbrook, Detlef in the sketch "The Hungry," Tonio Kröger, Klaus Heinrich in *Royal Highness*, Adrian Leverkühn in *Doctor Faustus* certainly are very lonely men; their loneliness is caused by their non-bourgeois feelings or their "formal existence." Yet Aschenbach's loneliness seems to be even greater than theirs.[6] His married daughter is the only living relative ever mentioned; but she is mentioned just once and plays no part whatever in the story. No friend is named, no fellow writer. What is perhaps more curious, no other living person beside Aschenbach is named except Tadzio and his friend Jaschu. Except for Tadzio, Aschenbach never thinks what he may mean to other persons or what other persons mean to him. Before coming to Venice, he does not seem to have any important human ties. He only lives for his art; he "sacrifices" his "life," and that in Mann's thinking means any possible friendship or love, to art. Unlike Tonio, he does not suffer from this separation and has no desire for communion with the masses. His loneliness is vanquished only in the orgiastic dream, where he is submerged in the mass of howling or panting men and women. He is "in them and with them" (431). This conquest of loneliness, however, does not make him happy. He feels ravaged, destroyed, degraded.

The old fop on the boat, who cavorts with the young men, calls Aschenbach his little sweetheart and has rouge on his cheeks, looks repulsive to Aschenbach. At first he seems utterly different from the dignified Aschenbach, but Aschenbach ultimately resembles him. It is perhaps ironical that posterity receives the news of Aschenbach's death with the "shock" of "respect" and not with disillusionment and indignation.

Tony Buddenbrook's insistence on "dignity" and prestige is humorous. The undignified death of the dignified Thomas Buddenbrook is ironic. In "Death in Venice," Mann wants to show that the artist's striving toward dignity is doomed to failure. The highly disciplined, aristocratic, and intellectual Aschenbach succumbs to the "irresistible temptation of the abyss," of chaos and irresponsibility. Yet, though it is hardly the height of dignity for a man of fifty to follow a boy of four-teen in the streets for hours on end, or to lean his forehead on the door of the room where this boy lives, it should be noted that Aschenbach never makes a vulgar gesture, never utters a vulgar word, never expresses a vulgar thought to Tadzio. Indeed, he does not even talk to him. Even his last days seem to be ennobled by thoughts of Plato. And his death, unlike that of Thomas Buddenbrook, is marked by dignity: He dies painlessly in the beach chair looking at the beautiful sea and the beauti-ful boy.

In the *Neue Rundschau,* where it was originally published, and in the *Collected Works* of 1960 the novella is divided into five chapters. Many a reader might think of the five acts of the traditional German tragedy, since Aschenbach seems to succumb to an inexorably tragic fate. One should not overlook, however, that the aging and tired writer only half-heartedly fights against his doom, that he finally chooses his self-destruction and, above all, that his death and the weeks preceding it do not detract or destroy anything from the excellence of his works, which are the truly great Aschenbach and which will long survive the Aschenbach in the flesh.

"Death in Venice" stands out as Mann's greatest achievement in the genre and as one of the most accomplished German stories of all times. Written in a masterly style, relatively short, but full of ideas, meanings, and overtones, it is a superb narra-tion of the rapid deterioration of a fine and disciplined mind, of love's progress in an aging person, a vivid description of the atmosphere and life in a resort, of mysterious Venice, of the impact of the plague, and an evocation of the ever-present lure and danger of evil and chaos. Though directed against art, it is a tribute to the beauty of the written word, the human body, and the ageless sea.

V Shots Against Mussolini

Mann wrote his short story "Mario and the Magician" in August, 1929, while vacationing at a Baltic resort. He utilized the experiences he had some time earlier in an Italian sea resort.

The narrator tells his story to a person who is neither named nor characterized. It is about a "tragic travel experience" which he had while vacationing with his wife and his two small children in Torre di Venere on the Tyrrhenian Sea. The style of the story, however, is never rambling, casual, informal, or hesitant, but literary throughout. The structure is clear and firm: the first part shows the irritating life at the resort; the second, an entertainment which continues and explains the general tenseness. The first paragraph points to the last.

The heat is extreme ("African"), and because of the discourtesy of a hotel manager the family moves from the Grand Hotel to a more modest pension. On the beach they are publicly insulted by a superpatriot because of an alleged impropriety of the little girl. Late one evening, the whole family attends a performance of the "magician" Cipolla. After some feats of mind-reading and some tricks with numbers and cards, Cipolla shows his great talent as a hypnotist. But after the hypnotized young Mario kisses the ugly conjurer, believing that he is kissing the girl he is in love with, he shoots Cipolla.

Mario, a shy, melancholy, but friendly waiter, who is known to the family from a garden café, only emerges toward the end, in the last eighth of the story. It is, therefore, remarkable that his name is the first component of the title, preceding even that of the magician. It is as if the author wanted to honor this modest young man, or at least the basic decency which he represents, and to raise him to the rank of a worthy or even superior antagonist of the powerful "illusionist."

It is useful to compare "Mario and the Magician" with the much earlier "Death in Venice." Both stories unfold exclusively, or for the most part, in an Italian resort during the holiday season. In both stories, the general atmosphere is unpleasant, and the stay at the resort should have been broken off. Both "artists" die at the end. Aschenbach's homoeroticism brings about his downfall, and the kiss which Cipolla forces Mario to give him, perhaps because of a homosexual inclination, is shortly followed by his collapse. Aschenbach's death may be called a "Liebestod," since the beauty of the beloved boy leads him to his death. But Cipolla, who pays with his life for the kiss of a young man, also dies of a "Liebestod" of sorts. In "Mario and the Magician," there are, as in "Death in Venice," names reminding us of classical antiquity: Venere, Mario, Ganymed; there is also a "classic weather" and the "sun of Homer" (533). The inhabitants of Venice live under the threat of an infectious disease, and the Italians in "Mario," too, pass "through something like a disease" (535), a highly infectious and dangerous one at that: fascism.

In "Death in Venice," the artist loses his extraordinary aristocratic dignity because of the impact of ordinary "life," sex, chaos, and irresponsibility. In "Mario and the Magician," ordinary citizens lose their dignity and their sense of responsibility and reality because of the illusions of extraordinary art. Both stories are indictments of art, although "Mario" is probably more an indictment of fascism. Both are devoid of humor and generally considered tragic; the original subtitle of "Mario" reads "Tragic Travel Experience."

Cipolla is a caricature of the artist, reminiscent of the "marked" men of Mann's earlier stories. He is a hunchback, drinks and smokes excessively, and suffers from an inferiority complex. He is called a "magician." It is to be noted that this was also Thomas Mann's nickname in his family from the time that he showed up at a masked ball in a magician's outfit. Some letters to members of his family he even signed "magician" (*Zauberer*, or Z). Cipolla's most remarkable achievement is to make people forget themselves and believe his lies. This power of illusion—Cipolla calls himself "illusionist"—is comparable to that of the great artist, painter, actor, or writer.

But Cipolla is more than just another of Mann's representations of the lonely, unhappy artist who is "different" and who is distrusted by the ordinary citizens. He is violently and outspokenly nationalistic and fascist. He manages to turn almost any topic into a subject of political propaganda. Using his strong will power and his rhetorical talent, and cracking his riding whip,

[127]

he forces men to dance on the stage, even a man who is resolved to resist and "to save the honor of the human race" (560).
Some victims enjoy their plight. One young man in particular, an
ecstatic youth, seems "quite content in his abject state, quite
pleased to be relieved of the burden of voluntary choice." Thus
Cipolla is an incarnation of the evil power which ugly fascism
held over the masses—especially the young, many of whom were
glad to escape from their personal freedom, their individual responsibility, and their sense of reality, in order to follow the
commands of the leader and to act as the others did.

Mann may have had the prophetic feeling that the apparently
irresistible attraction of fascism could only end in violence.
Cipolla's "entertainment," that lasts much too long, as the narrator repeatedly stresses, only ends when he is shot by the
young man whose deep and unhappy love he had mocked.
The end is a genuine relief for the narrator. Five times he uses
the word "end" in the last paragraph of the German original.
"An end of horror, a fatal end. And yet a liberation."

The narrator makes it clear in the very first paragraph, where
the "horrible end" is announced, that Cipolla is more than a
"dreadful being." He "incorporates in so fateful and so humanly
impressive a way, all the peculiar evilness of the situation as a
whole." The "situation" means not only the "extreme, frightful,
relentless" heat of the sun (533), but also the "byzantinism" of
the hotel manager, and, particularly, the newly sharpened
patriotism and xenophobia of many Italian guests, the phrases
about the greatness and honor of Italy, the outburst of patriotic
morality leading to the intervention of the police against the
father of a little girl who was naked on the beach for a few
minutes.

The revulsion which the author feels toward the blind and
stupid nationalism of the middle-class vacationists and the sur-
render of one's will to strong but evil power is coupled with his
negative attitude toward the "occult." In the early twenties,
Mann was fascinated by spiritism and telepathy and visited some
spiritualist séances in Munich. As he wrote in his essay "Experiences of the Occult" and indirectly in the *Magic Mountain,* he
was puzzled and even sickened by what he saw. There was too
much humbug and ambiguity inherent in those strange experiences. That unpleasant impression is even "deepened" when
a Cipolla is responsible for it (552).

Thus, the novella of a little mountebank's death of 1929 has connections with the short stories about marked men of the 1890's, with "Death in Venice," the great novella of a master's death of 1912, and with the *Magic Mountain,* the great novel about the education of an average man through disease and death of 1924; but "Mario and the Magician" is, above all, one of Mann's earliest pronouncements against the deadly menace of political mass hypnosis and an overheated and overbearing nationalism.

VI *Other Stories*

"Disillusionment" (1896) is the earliest novella which Mann included in his collected stories and works. In Venice, an unnamed stranger, a lonely and queer man, tells the narrator of the problem that afflicts his life: He is disillusioned by everything that life can offer, joy as well as anguish, for everything is limited. He has been disappointed by nature, art, and love; and he thinks that he will be disappointed by death, too. He always sees "the horizon." Like the hero of Goethe's *The Sorrows of Young Werther,* a book from which he quotes a paragraph, he longs in vain for infinity. He blames his painful disillusionment on his education, on the "big words" used by priests and poets, which "called up infinite emotions in him" and made him expect great things in life.

Mann, who was about to write *Buddenbrooks,* the ironic, pessimistic, and realistic masterpiece, shares the stranger's rejection of "pathetic optimism" and big words which are based on the ignorance of real life. He, too, suffered from the limitations and boundaries of human life, which explains his enthusiastic endorsement of Schopenhauer's pessimism that teaches the illusory nature of boundaries and horizons. But, unlike the stranger, he sometimes joyfully experienced infinity, at least in his feelings for the sea.

The protagonist of "Little Herr Friedemann" (1897) is a hunchback, because his nurse let him drop when he was a month old. He has renounced love and happiness, and leads a quiet life, getting some enjoyment out of nature, music, literature, and the theater. At thirty, the tranquillity of his life is shattered. He falls madly in love with the elegant Gerda. She encourages his feelings, perhaps because, for some reason, she herself is unhappy. But when she scornfully rejects his advances, he commits suicide by drowning.

The irony is already inherent in the title; in the "little," in "Friede," which means peace, and perhaps even in "mann," since the protagonist is not much of a man. The harmless hunchback highly values his "Seelenfrieden," his peace of mind; but he cannot maintain this state because of the cruelty of life. The sad story begins with the irony of the title and literally ends with "laughter." The title is repeated again and again in the story, a special application of the leitmotif.

Gerda, with her red hair, the blue shadows around her eyes, her musical interests, and her elusiveness, reappears in *Buddenbrooks*, as do Friedemann's sisters, with their names (Friederike, Henriette, and Pfiffi), their spinsterhood, and their remarks about other girls' engagements. The destruction of the peace of mind of a lonely man by late and almost grotesque love is again shown in "Death in Venice."

Like the lonely stranger in "Disillusionment," the outsider in "The Dilettante" (1897) tells his life story; and, like the stranger again, all that he feels for life as a whole is "disgust." Thirty years old, like Herr Friedemann when he takes his life, he contemplates committing suicide. His childhood and youth recall Mann's: the life in the little old city with its irregular gabled streets and Gothic churches; the patrician house where he grows up; the father, a sound and respected business man; the musical mother; the musical dramas which he performs with his puppet theater; the poor work he does at school; and the liquidation of the firm after his father's death.

The narrator, who remains anonymous like the "disillusioned" stranger, has talents for acting, writing, painting, and playing the piano, but he can use them only to amuse people as a sort of clown or "Bajazzo," as the German title of the story reads. He has always lacked the self-discipline to cultivate any talent systematically and purposefully. As a scorned outsider, he ends by living an outwardly peaceful life (echoes of Herr Friedemann again), getting some enjoyment out of reading new books and going to concerts.

The mocking disregard which a society girl, with whom he has fallen in love, shows for him, destroys whatever happiness and self-confidence he still has. He knows that he cuts a "wretched and ridiculous figure" and thinks that there is "only one kind of unhappiness: to suffer the loss of pleasure in oneself" (49).

In "The Dilettante," Mann shows the effects of decadence, a phenomenon that intrigued many minds at the end of the century. It is decadence that accounts for the young man's total lack of will power and a sense of responsibility and direction. The story may also express Mann's early fear of artistic sterility and his long-held conviction that the artist is an outsider and a sort of clown, whom the "normal" do not respect and who does not respect himself.

The "puzzling and sinister" story entitled "Tobias Minder-nickel" (1897) is about another queer and lonely man. He is followed in the street by a laughing mob of children, and bows humbly to people. Only once, when he helps a wounded boy to his feet, does he look different; he holds himself erect, and there is an expression of joy on his face.

He acquires a dog, treats him with love, and feels happy when Esau obeys his orders, shows affection or is wounded, but treats him without mercy when the dog does not obey or runs away. One day when Esau escapes from him and jumps mockingly around, he plunges a big knife deep into the dog's chest. The next minute, he stammers "My poor dog," lays his face against Esau's dead body, and weeps "bitter tears."

Queerness becomes a pathological case. The weak-willed and humble Tobias, defeated by life, taunted by everybody, needs somebody who is weaker than he is. He craves for love and is capable of pity and affection, but becomes furious and dangerous when his affection is ignored.

Mindernickel's excessive insecurity and humility is perhaps surpassed by the fat lawyer Jacoby in "Little Lizzy" (1897), an elephantine "colossus of a man," whose obsequiousness is almost "crawling" and who despises himself. When a porter with a hand cart runs over his foot, Jacoby takes off his hat and stutters: "I beg your pardon." He loves his wife, the sensuous and pretty Amra, who has an affair with Alfred Läutner, a young musician.

The cruel Amra forces her husband to perform at a large party. Wearing a blond wig and a shapeless garment, the lawyer, in a choked voice, sings "Little Lizzy," a composition by

Läutner, who, with Amra at his side, accompanies Jacoby at the piano. The audience, gazing at the lamentable figure on the stage and at the guilty pair at the piano, is horror-stricken. When the lawyer's gaze travels from the pair to the audience, a sudden awareness seems to flash across his puffy face, and he collapses. The physician's only comment is the short "Aus" ("All over").

Life's cruelty and man's suffering are portrayed with cold irony and vivid precision. Music has often been considered by Mann as a dangerous force; and it is the music of the little song that opens the lawyer's eyes and kills him. The detailed description of the little song is the first of Mann's many analyses of compositions which show his great musical sensitivity and knowledge.

"The Wardrobe" (1899) occupies a unique position among Mann's novellas, indeed among all his works, because of its almost Surrealist atmosphere. Albrecht van der Qualen, a man between twenty-five and thirty years of age, whose physicians give him only a few more months to live, for no apparent reason leaves his train at an unnamed railroad station, though he had bought a ticket for Florence. He takes a modest apartment in a poor section of a little German town. In the wardrobe of this apartment, a beautiful naked girl often appears and tells him sad stories or poems. "Two walked on the heath and her head lay on his shoulder . . . So it began. And often it was in verse, rhyming in an incomparably sweet and flowing way" (77). Whenever he gives in to his desire, she does not come back for several nights. At the end of the story, the possibility is left open that he may have dreamed it all in his first-class carriage. "It is all uncertain."

"Everything must be in the air," the last sentence, is Albrecht's motto, and apparently the narrator's motto as well. He refuses to say how long Albrecht has stayed in the town because, as he says, nobody "would care for a wretched number." Albrecht has no watch and is not interested in knowing what time or what day, or even year, it is. This deliberate adoption of timelessness by the incurable protagonist heralds the atmosphere in the sanitarium of *The Magic Mountain*.

It is impossible to say what the girl really "means" or whether she is supposed to mean anything (the Muse, for instance, or the beauty of Heine's, Storm's, or Neoromantic works). With all the calculated uncertainties and mysteries, there are some detailed realistic descriptions, such as those of Albrecht's face and the apartment. Ironically, the furniture, particularly the wardrobe itself and the three chairs, were Mann's own. There are also echoes of Lübeck: the old gate with two massive towers, and the bridge with statues on the railing.

Albrecht is an outsider, "as probably no man has ever been before." He has no business and no goal. It is perhaps significant that he declines to put up at the "Hotel zum braven Mann," for a "braver Mann" is an honest member of society. The "story," with its blend of lyrical softness and precise description, fantasy and realism, has a fascination all its own, regardless of all the possible biographical or philosophical interpretations.

In "The Way to the Churchyard" (1901), Praisegod Piepsam walks to the cemetery in order to visit the graves of his wife and children. He wears old and shabby clothes, has a huge Adam's apple and a "knobby" nose that glows with unnatural redness. Piepsam is quite unhappy. He has lost his job because of his habitual drunkenness. When a young and carefree bicyclist passes him on the walk, Piepsam insults him and tries to stop him. He flies into a rage, collapses, and is taken away by an ambulance.

This lonely, wretched, and ridiculous outsider has Jacoby's and the "dilettante's" self-contempt. It is perhaps no accident that he works at an insurance company, as Mann temporarily did in Munich. The cyclist has blond hair and blue eyes, which in young Mann's picture album signifies a harmless, normal, and healthy life that does not care about the unhappy outsiders. He is repeatedly called "Life."

Although the story is basically sad, it displays a great deal of irony and a certain playfulness. The narrator, for instance, declines to describe a carriage because there is no little dog in it.

There is an odd-looking outsider in "Gladius Dei" (1902), too, but he is a fighter for an ideal, not a drunk. The story takes place in Munich. The city is radiant with the splendor of a fine day in early June, which enhances the beauty of its many palaces, monuments, and parks. It throbs with the joy of life, love, painting, music, architecture, the theater, and literature. Hieronymus is the only unhappy-looking pedestrian. "The hood of his ample black cloak is drawn over his head and frames his haggard cheeks." Seen in profile, his face looks like an old painting preserved at Florence in a cloister cell "whence once a protest issued against life and her triumphs" (184). The name, appearance, and thoughts of the young man foreshadow Girolamo Savonarola in Mann's "Fiorenza."

A crowd is gathered in front of an art dealer's store to look at the photograph of a painting depicting the Madonna. Hieronymus sees that the Virgin is quite sensuous and that she suggests sex rather than religion. Wherever he goes, the picture of the Madonna follows him. On the third night, a command from on high comes to him to lift his voice against the frivolity, blasphemy, and arrogance of beauty.

When he asks the owner of the store to destroy the photograph, together with "all the statues and busts the sight of which plunges the beholder into sin, the vases and ornaments, these shameless revivals of paganism, these elegantly bound volumes of erotic verse" (192), he is thrown out of the store. But he does not despair. In his mind, he sees the masked costumes of the artist balls, the decorations, vases, art objects, the nude statues, the portraits of famous beauties, the art brochures heaped in a pyramid and going up in flames amid loud exultations from the people. And in the dark thunderstorm cloud he sees a fiery sword towering over the joyous city. He murmurs, "Gladius dei super terram, cito et velociter."

The contrast between the easy-going, art-loving, happy people, their banter, jokes, and colorful life, and the deadly serious and fanatical man is very striking. The contrast is also symbolized by the "rose-bound scepter which art, swaying the destinies of the town, stretches above it" (183) and the flaming sword of the spirit which Hieronymus sees in the sky. Spirit, which in some of Mann's works, such as "Tonio Kröger," is united with art or synonymous with it, is here opposed to it. Mann, who, at the time of writing the story, was living in Munich, may have been uneasy about the superficiality and *joie de vivre* of the artists, the artists' models, and of people in general. The tolerant city seemed to ignore misery and suffering, and scorn morality.

Hieronymus is not opposed to art as such, he says, but to art as a "conscienceless delusion lending itself to reinforce the allurements of the flesh," instead of being "the holy torch which turns its light upon all the frightful depths, all the shameful and woeful abysses of life" (191). Thus art as a moral force, as a means of redemption is upheld, while art for its own sake or for the sake of mere enjoyment is rejected.

The descriptive phrase that is repeated most often is perhaps indicative of the young man's being "wrapped in his own thoughts" (183) and of his determination: He is "holding his wide cloak together with both hands from inside" (184, 185, twice on 186, 187, 188). Other descriptive repetitions are indicative of the opposite world: the "bleating laughter" of a customer in the art store (187, 189, 190, 191) and the "little girls, the pretty, rather plump type, with the brunette bandeaux, the too large feet, and the unobjectionable morals" (181, 184, 187).

"The Hungry" (1902), called a "study," is a short finger exercise for "Tonio Kröger." The writer Detlef, "struck by the sense of his own superfluity," leaves a gay party and the girl with whom he is in love. He is one of the lonely dreamers who cherish a hidden yearning for the harmless, simple, real, normal, banal, and respectable life. But he knows that warm life is in eternal opposition to the spirit, that he alienates the blond and blue-eyed, and that he cannot escape the curse: "You may not live, you must create" (170).

He would cry, if there were tears in the world of "rigid desolation, ice, spirit, and art." As in other of Mann's outsiders, there is a mixture of self-pity and self-contempt in Detlef. At the end of the story, he recognizes that he is a brother of the wretched beggar outside the theater. They are both "hungry" with envy and longing for a happy life. Detlef now even thinks that all men are brothers, since all are "creatures of the restless suffering Will." His last words are: "Little children, love one another!" Thus, as in "Tonio Kröger," love finally somehow bridges the eternal gulf between spirit (art) and life.

"The Infant Prodigy," published in 1903—at the same time as "Tonio Kröger" and "Tristan"—is a sketch about a child prodigy's sucessful piano recital in an unnamed city. The eight-year old boy with an impossibly long Greek name, whose program is made up of his own compositions, has all the qualities and defects of an adult artist. He has genuine inspiration and talent, but there is also a lack of dignity, something of a showman, a charlatan, or a clown in him. He despises the public for its lack of taste and understanding. He wears a bow in his hair and greets the audience as would a woman. Apparently this is meant to imply that the artist is not a real man, as Tonio Kröger once puts it. It also reminds one of the beardless Spinell and the bisexual Aschenbach and Leverkühn, as well as of Felix Krull, who excites both sexes.

Most of the spectators are quite enthusiastic about the child, but the more knowledgeable ones have some reservations about his originality or sincerity. Mann gives brief and mostly satirical glimpses of a vain critic, a spinster piano teacher, an old princess, an aristocratic young lady and her two officer brothers, an adolescent and oversensitive girl, an impresario, a businessman with a parrot's nose, an unkempt girl artist and her somber boy friend. Like the child, he is somewhat contemptuous of their "people's brains," their desire to be fooled, and their herd instinct. The unkempt girl's statement, "We are all child prodigies," seems to be his idea, too. The sketch caricatures the successful artist and the public's reaction to him.

"A Gleam" (1904) takes place at a gay party in an officers' casino. Anna is jealous of her husband, Baron Harry, a handsome lady-killer, who, toward the end of the party, gives his wedding ring to Emmy, one of the fifth-class chorus girls who are its great attraction. Emmy returns the ring to Anna and kisses her hand, and Anna has "a gleam" of happiness. "For it brings happiness . . . when the two worlds between which longing plies touch each other for one fleeting, illusory moment."

Anna represents spirit, Emmy (and Harry) life. Emmy is not interested in Harry but in a lonely, shy, and clumsy writer—another representative of spirit—because he looks poetic, noble, as if he belonged to a different world. The writer, in his turn, is attracted to Anna, but she does not pay any attention to him, because he is of her own world, as Tonio Kröger does not care for Magdalena, the intellectual girl who loves him.

In "At the Prophet's" (1904), a disciple of the "prophet" Daniel reads on Good Friday a proclamation that is a nebulous and megalomaniac mixture of brutality and weakness, of militarism and a Messianic religion, of sermons, laws, prophecies, and exhortations, of Nietzsche and Stefan George. "Christus

Imperator Maximus" enrolls troops for the subjection of the globe. He exacts obedience, poverty, and chastity. Buddha, Alexander, Napoleon, and Jesus were his "humble forerunners." He "delivers for plundering—the world."

The sketch is copied from life. Among the thirteen, mostly odd listeners in the strangely furnished attic of a tenement house is the well-dressed and polite short-story writer, who, as a leitmotif assures, is "on good terms with life," an obvious, slightly ironic self-portrait of the author of "Tonio Kröger." Daniel's model was Ludwig Derleth, a disciple of George and author of *Proclamations*. He was to reappear forty years later in *Doctor Faustus* as Daniel zur Höhe, a forerunner of Nazism. The exquisite Sonia, whom the writer loves and whose elegant mother is one of the visitors, is Katja Pringsheim, who became Mann's wife in the following year. The mocking realism of the descriptions and the occasional social banter form an effective contrast to the madness of Daniel's message.

The conflict between ascetic moralism and sensual aestheticism, which unfolds vividly in "Gladius Dei," is treated once more two years later in "Fiorenza" (1905). Although "Fiorenza" has dramatic form and was performed in several theaters, it usually appears together with the stories, for Mann's only play lacks dramatic pace and power.

The action of this three-act play takes place in a villa near Florence on the afternoon of April 8, 1492. Lorenzo dei Medici is gravely ill. He has ruled Florence with cruelty and cunning, without regard for law and virtue (250), but he has generously patronized the arts. His adversary, the Dominican Girolamo Savonarola, preaches against the revival of paganism and the idolization of beauty. He has an immense following, and the future is his. From the first word of the play, he is spiritually on the stage, although he only appears in the last two scenes. Significantly for the importance of the number seven in Mann's work, he and Lorenzo clash in the seventh, and last, scene of the third act.

The men, though radically different in their outlook on life, are in some respects alike. They are both heroes after Mann's liking: men who had to surmount their own weaknesses. "He who is weak, but of so glowing a spirit that even so he wins the garland—he is a hero" (235). Both were and are weak, ugly, and sick. Both have been eager for absolute power and despise the "people."

Their ideals and lives are explained psychologically. Had Lorenzo been born handsome, he would never have made himself the lord of beauty (268). That Savonarola became a prophet of pure spirit, an ascetic and pessimistic critic of life is explained by the fact that, as a young man, he was rejected by the beautiful Fiore. Fiore, who is a symbol of life, beauty, and Florence, became Lorenzo's mistress, but shows increasing interest in Savonarola.

Though a saint, Savonarola is an artist, at least insofar as he is an orator. Like other artists in Mann's fiction, he does not live apart from his work. "I live only in my pulpit," he tells Fiore (262). At the end, after Lorenzo's death, Savonarola goes "into his destiny," unafraid of the dangers, unwilling to renounce power. He is the real hero of the play and of Mann's own pessimistic moralism. He has "made morality, long considered only boring and ridiculous, possible again" (211-212). It will supplant decadent aestheticism. In his early plan of 1900, Mann called the play "Savonarola."

The artists who often crowd the stage are treated with irony, if not sarcasm. They are vain, unscrupulous, childish; liars, boasters, sycophants, fools, swindlers, and clowns. They have no religion or conviction. Money, reputation, and artistic technique are the only things that matter to them. One senses Mann's rejection of the Bohemian way of life and of the cult of beauty, which pervades everything—houses, furniture, utensils, streets, and parades—but closes the eyes and the mind to the wretchedness and ugliness in life.

The play suffers from its static nature and its verboseness. Pico once tells a story that takes six pages (202-207). One of his subsequent remarks is three pages long. Leone even narrates a novella. The play also suffers from a certain vagueness. Words such as "spirit," "knowledge," and "art" are stretched to cover confusingly different things.

Like a classical play, "Fiorenza" observes the unities of time, place, and "action." Occasionally, it also displays iambic pentameters and proverbial sayings à la Schiller: "Hindrance is the will's best friend" (268), "Fame is the school of scorn" (269). Mann's excursion into the dramatic realm is one of his least successful ventures.

"A Weary Hour" ("Schwere Stunde") was written for an anniversary, one hundred and fifty years after Friedrich Schiller's death. The great German dramatist has a "difficult hour" during a December night. He is plagued by his chronic cold and serious pains in the chest and beset by doubts about the play he is working on (apparently *Wallenstein*) and about his future as a writer. His whole life has been a constant and wearying struggle against poverty and pains. On the other hand, his only peer is Goethe, whom he "loves and hates," for whom things, life as well as writing, are much easier, but to whom, in some respects, he feels superior. He finally triumphs over his brooding, goes back to work, to "define, eliminate, fashion, and complete. . . . And from his soul . . . new works struggled upward to birth and, taking shape, gave out light and sound, ringing and shimmering, and giving hint of their infinite origin."

Schiller is portrayed by Mann as a "moralist of achievement," as a man who surmounts the greatest obstacles outside and within himself, who has to fight against poverty, illness, darkness, and chaos, who sacrifices himself for his work, who can never be really happy, for whom every thought, every sentence means discipline and self-control, and for whom life is but a succession of "weary hours." But Schiller also displays a firm belief in his greatness and immortality and to a high degree shows the egoism and narcissism which, according to Mann, are characteristic of the artist. Mann's Schiller is a lonely, proud, and disciplined artist like Tonio Kröger, Gustav Aschenbach, and Adrian Leverkühn, who also sacrifice their happiness and make the highest demands on their work.

The short "story" has no plot to speak of. Most of it is in the nature of an interior monologue, even though generally the grammatical third person is used, and not the first. The Germans call it "erlebte Rede." It is difficult not to compare the Schiller of the "Weary Hour" with the Goethe of the much larger *Beloved Returns*, where Goethe, Schiller's friend and counterpart, has a succession of interior monologues and where, again, the themes of greatness, loneliness, sickness, work, and sacrifice are sounded.

Fifty years after the "Weary Hour," Mann wrote what turned out to be his swan song, the "Essay on Schiller," "dedicated in love to the memory" of a poet whom he loved throughout his life and whose idealism and gentle but mighty will, as he said in the conclusion of his essay, should be an inspiration to humanity.

The title of "The Blood of the Walsungs" (1905) refers, like that of "Tristan," to an opera by Wagner. It, too, is ironical. Spinell is no Tristan, and the twins Siegmund and Sieglinde Aarenhold do not have the blood of the Walsungs in their veins. The two see a performance of *Die Walküre*, where their name-sakes, also brother and sister, meet incestuously. Back to their luxurious home, they do likewise; and when Sieglinde mentions her fiancé, whom she is to marry the following week, her brother-lover replies—concluding the novella—"He ought to be grateful to us. His existence will be a little less trivial from now on."

This cynical remark is only one of the many bristling utterances of the twins. Although rich, cultured, and spoiled, they are on the defense because of their Jewish looks and because of the Jewish origin of their father, who "by means of a bold and shrewd enterprise had diverted an inexhaustible stream of gold into his affairs" (301). The two, obviously identical twins, love and admire each other, hold hands all the time, caress and kiss each other, but have only sharp comments or arrogant contempt for everybody else.

The contrast between over-refined decadence and normality, apparent in *Buddenbrooks,* "Tonio Kröger," and "The Dilettante," is once again stressed. The normal, active, and rather harmless people are blond and blue-eyed Germans, such as the boring Von Beckerath, Sieglinde's fiancé; but the decadent and marked ones have dark hair and dark eyes.

Siegmund's dilettantism and artistic sterility recall "The Dilettante." Siegmund dabbles in painting, but suffers from his inability to be creative. His effeminate narcissism is that of Spinell. Like Spinell, Siegmund attentively looks at himself in the mirror. The disgraceful incest of the "graceful" twins heralds the much later *Holy Sinner;* their caustic remarks and their extraordinary life of loneliness and luxury point forward to Imma Spoelmann in *Royal Highness.*

Oddly enough, Mann used the Pringsheim family as his model for some motives of this novella. Katja Pringsheim, whom he married in 1905, had a twin brother Klaus. Their father was a wealthy professor of mathematics of Jewish origin, who, like Mr. Aarenhold, collected books. He also was an ardent Wagnerian, which would explain the names Siegmund and Sieglinde. Like the Aarenhold children, the Pringsheim children had their own libraries. These and other similarities between the two families, however, are greatly outweighed by the differences. Mann may have indulged in some private teasing and overshot his mark. In order to forestall any misunderstandings and hasty identifications, and perhaps also anti-Semitic or anti-anti-Semitic reactions, he withdrew the novella just before it was to be published in *Die Neue Rundschau.* It was published years later, in a special luxury edition and in a French and an English translation. Although the German text was added to the collected stories only after Mann's death, "The Blood of the Walsungs" ranks among his best novellas.

"The Railway Accident" (1907) is a humorous account of a minor train collision. The narrator, obviously Mann himself, travels first-class from Munich to Dresden, where he is scheduled to give a lecture. After the derailment, he worries most about his manuscripts, which are in the baggage car. The story boasts a few small and ironical sketches of passengers and railway employees.

"The Fight Between Jappe and Do Escobar" (1911) is a sensitive glimpse into the world of fourteen-year-old boys, who on the beach of Travemünde witness a "duel" between the muscular Jappe and the wiry and exotic Do Escobar under the supervision of Mr. Knaak, a ballet master familiar to readers of "Tonio Kröger." The boys' fascination with honor, violence, and male strength is shared by the narrator himself, although he is rather shy and "unwarlike."

"A Man and His Dog," written in 1918, is a hundred pages long. It was Mann's first work of fiction in seven years. The "idyll," composed in the first person, is about his dog Bashan—

the German name is Bauschan—, a German pointer, who, with his "peasant-like" vigor and normality, is quite different from his predecessor, an aristocratic and crazy collie.

With sympathy and benevolent irony, Mann describes his "friend," and his "friend's" apathy, excitement, despondency, mockery, exultation, boredom, embarrassment, and dissatisfaction. Bashan enjoys mostly the opportunities to chase mice, hares, pheasants, ducks, and seagulls, and does it with zest though with little success. We encounter a number of humorous episodes, such as that of the sheep which falls in love with the dog, that of the hare who jumps up on Mann, and that of the dialogue between Bashan and Mann, who needs more than a page to justify himself before his critical "friend."

The description of the "hunting ground" on the outskirts of Munich, with its trees and flowers, is unusually detailed for Mann; he was helped by a botanist, a neighbor of his. The idyll contains an important passage on Mann's nature mysticism, his mystical feelings being aroused by the sight and sound of water, by a brook, and especially by the sea.

"Song of the Child," published in 1919, is an idyll in hexameters. Mann imitated Goethe's *Hermann und Dorothea*, with which his own work shares, among other things, the background of war and revolution, but whose scope, excellence, and popularity it is far from approaching. The "Song," consisting of nine parts and written in the first person, also offers general observations and digressions, such as those on the difference between a poet and a writer and on the relationship between Lübeck and Venice, but it is mainly devoted to Mann's baby, his fifth and favorite child, Elisabeth, who was born in April, 1918. The last part, one third of the "Song," describes her baptism.

Mann explains his use of the hexameter by the fact that this meter, whose spirit and sound, as he thinks, can already be felt in some passages of the canine idyll, is helpful in the leisurely description of domestic happiness. His own hexameters, however, are too uneven to be of any help. Mann expressed his fatherly feelings for Elisabeth much more effectively a few years later in "Disorder and Early Sorrow."

The two autobiographical idylls are important because they were Mann's first creative writings in a long time, and because they deal with subjects mostly ignored in the *Magic Mountain:*

animals, little children, and domestic life. They are, as he himself said, products of the deeply felt need for a change, for peace,
serenity, and affection. This need is understandable after the
long years of the war and of his bitter political and personal
polemics.

"Disorder and Early Sorrow" (1925) is one of Mann's most
popular stories. He "improvised it for relaxation" after the
long and strenuous work on *The Magic Mountain* and published
it in *Die Neue Rundschau* on the occasion of his fiftieth birthday. The "early sorrow" is felt by the five-year old Ellie. Max
Hergesell, a pleasant and good-looking student, has jocularly
danced with her at the house party and she cannot stop crying
or fall asleep until Max visits her in her bedroom. The "disorder" is the inflation, the postwar shortages and privations, the
way of life of the young generation in Germany, specifically in
Munich, around 1922 and 1923. To the professor, his feelings
for his daughter Ellie represent order and timelessness among
the disorder, lawlessness, and irrelevance of his time, but Ellie
herself seems to be seized by the very "disorder."

Dr. Cornelius has pangs of jealousy because his little daughter,
whom he loves above everything, has "fallen in love" with
another man. He also feels out of place in the postwar world.
While the young enjoy the present and look forward to the
future, he is immersed in the past, not only because of his age
but also because he is a professor of history, whose "heart
belongs to the coherent and disciplined historic past" (506).
Ironically, the whole novella, which is told from the professor's point of view, is narrated in the present tense. Yet, Mann
had just finished *The Magic Mountain,* which calls the narrator
the "conjurer of the past tense."

Dr. Cornelius is, of course, Mann himself, who had a professorial appearance and bent. Eleanor is Mann's favorite
child Elisabeth. The other Cornelius children, Ingrid, Bert, and
Snapper, resemble Erika, Klaus, and Michael Mann. The ages
of the members of the Mann family and those of their equivalents
in the Cornelius family are identical. Contrary to her role in
Royal Highness, but in line with "Mario and the Magician,"
Katja Mann is not much in evidence.

The ambitions, successes, failures, jokes, slang, dances, and
peculiarities of the young men and women (students, actors,

employees, and servants), the gulf between the generations, the devaluation of the money and of the bourgeois tradition, parental love and worries, and, above all, the behavior of little children are rendered with skill, charm, and humor, with malice toward none and gentle irony toward all. Mann escaped the Scylla of bitterness and the Charybdis of sentimentality. The professor is no pedant, and even those readers who find Mann ponderous in his great works take delight in this professorial sketch.

"The Transposed Heads" (1940) is based on a Sanskrit legend reported by Heinrich Zimmer—to whom the English translation is dedicated—and on other Indian sources; but the action following the transposition of the heads, many details, and some basic themes are Mann's own.

In the temple of the Great Mother Kâlî the young intellectual merchant Shridaman cuts off his own head because his beautiful wife Sita is in love with his friend, the handsome and strong cowherd Nanda. Nanda, who never wanted to survive Shridaman, lops off his head, too. When Sita is about to commit suicide, Kâlî tells her to rejoin the heads and bodies of her husband and his friend; they would live again. In her haste, or out of an unconscious desire to have a perfect lover, Sita affixes the heads to the wrong bodies. A hermit, whom the three choose as their arbitrator, decides that Sita must live with the man who has Shridaman's head and Nanda's body. Sita is very happy since this new Shridaman is perfection itself, spirit as well as beauty and vigor. But slowly Shridaman's looks turn common and Sita starts dreaming of Nanda again. When her son is four years old, she leaves her husband and joins Nanda, who is now a hermit. With the years, the Nanda-head has become more refined and the Shridaman-body stronger and more beautiful. On the morning of the night which Sita and Nanda spend together, Shridaman joins them. In order to put an end to their dilemma, Nanda and Shridaman kill each other, and Sita joins them on the funeral pyre. Her handsome, intelligent, and cultured, though near-sighted, son becomes a king's reader.

Mann labelled this "Indian legend" a "metaphysical jest." Some parts seem purely metaphysical; others—more numerous— purely farcical. The metaphysics—the illusory character of the world, the problems of individuation and identity—leans on Indian religion and on Schopenhauer. Though the basic frustration of human life, the five suicides (or three suicides and two murders), and the attempted suicide are hardly comic, the legend as a whole is very humorous, particularly after the transposition of the heads, when familiar metaphors and phrases involving the head, the face, and the body acquire new and comic meaning. One particularly farcical episode is that of the old hermit and his fascination with sex.

Mann may have been drawn to the legend by the grotesqueness of the transposition and the ensuing problem of identity, a problem which he had dealt with in *Joseph* and in essays like those on Kleist's *Amphitryon* and on "Freud and the Future." Once he said that his story was "mischievous, oscillating," and that it did not yield a definite meaning.[7] It seems to play with several basic ideas and themes. The story shows, first of all, the impossibility of achieving a synthesis of spirit and beauty in life. It also proves that love, which "always wants the whole," i.e., perfection, can never be satisfied, that a few years change even an ideal man and lover into a mere husband, perhaps also that woman can or must break up even an ideal friendship between men, and that she is always dreaming of an ideal lover.

Mann himself identified the triangle of the story with Tonio, Hans, and Inge of "Tonio Kröger." There is, to be sure, in both stories the opposition of spirit and beauty, but Nanda is a sincere and admiring friend, not a superficial Hans. Unlike Inge, who does not care for Tonio, Sita loves Shridaman; and, most importantly, Shridaman is not an outsider like Tonio.

The legend consists of twelve parts and is about a hundred pages long. The narrative technique is that of *The Magic Mountain* and *Joseph*. Indologists find that Mann's descriptions of Indian life and landscape are authentic. The style is mixed as in *Joseph* and other of his late works. Use is made of rather abstract terms, occasional anglicisms, and archaic as well as colloquial expressions. As in *Joseph*, we find here and there alliteration, rhymes, and puns.

Mann called his Indian legend a "divertissement" or "intermezzo,"[8] which indeed it is, written between two weighty volumes, *Joseph in Egypt* and *Joseph the Provider*. It is both amusing and confusing, but it has not contributed to the author's fame.

"The Tables of the Law" (1943) was written as a commissioned introduction for a book containing the contributions of ten famous writers, each about one of the Ten Commandments.

Mann read Goethe's essay "Israel in the Desert," Freud's *Moses and Monotheism* and the Pentateuch. The "Sinaic novella" in twenty chapters, which he wrote in less than two months, seemed to him a "natural postlude to the *Joseph* story" (*Story*, 15). He gave it the title "Das Gesetz" ("The Law"), because he was referring not only to the Decalogue, but to moral law and civilization in general.

From Freud he took the idea that Moses was the son of an Egyptian princess,[9] and that he chose a people of his own. Moses' features resemble less Michelangelo's famous statue of Moses, which fascinated Freud a great deal, than Michelangelo himself; and his difficult and often desperate task of creating a civilized people out of barbarians is repeatedly compared to the work of a sculptor, "toiling laboriously over refractory material."

Mann's Moses is not only the author of the Decalogue, but, curiously enough, also the inventor of the Hebrew alphabet, which, according to the novella, is the first one that could be used for all languages. The moral sculptor Moses stands for the spiritual and intellectual leaders, the artists, whose difficult and necessary work is constantly endangered by thoughtlessness, stupidity, cowardice, sloth, materialism, ugliness, and barbarism. He also experiences, like other artistic figures created by Mann, loneliness in school and in life.

Even more than in *The Holy Sinner,* miracles, such as the ten plagues, or the stick which changes into a serpent, or the Red Sea which recedes to let the Israelites pass, are rationalized. God mostly speaks through Moses' thoughts. The treatment of the Biblical characters is not warm and humorous as in *Joseph,* but is carried out in the manner of a cool Voltairean mockery.

The pace is much faster and the style simpler and more prosaic than in *Joseph.* Alliteration and rhymes are less frequent. Mann was serious about the importance and dignity of moral law. Moses' concluding curse against the present-day wretches (i.e., Hitler and consorts) "to whom power was given to profane His work" came from his own heart, Mann asserts, and "leaves no doubt of the militant intent of the otherwise somewhat frivolous little thing" (*Story*, 16-17).

The novella "The Black Swan" was Mann's first work after his return from the United States to Switzerland in 1952. It is based on an actual event. True to his working habits, Mann asked a doctor for specific medical information and some inhabitants of Düsseldorf for topographical data and Rhenish expressions. The novella, about one hundred and twenty pages long, was finished in April, 1953, and generally met with a poor reception. Mann himself did not value it highly. It is, however, slowly gaining recognition.

Rosalie von Tümmler, an attractive widow over fifty years of age, who lives in the Düsseldorf of the 1920's, falls in love with Ken Keaton, a twenty-four-year-old American war veteran, who tutors her son. A few hours before their rendezvous is to take place, she is taken to the hospital, where a cancer of the womb and other organs is diagnosed and where she dies shortly after the operation. She had joyfully taken a bleeding caused by her disease for the resumption of her menstruation.

The German title of this novella, "Die Betrogene" ("The Deceived Woman"), points to Mann's original intention to show Nature as a deceiver, as he does in the experiments of Adrian's father in *Doctor Faustus*. "The Deceived Woman" (1953) was actually followed by *Felix Krull*, the deceiving man (1954).[10] But Rosalie, a great lover of life, dies reconciled with Nature. "Never say that Nature deceived me. Death is a great instrument of life, and if for me it borrowed the guise of resurrection and of the joy of love, it was not deceit, but goodness and grace" (140). The novella has changed its direction; the bitterness over Nature's demonic cruelty is replaced by serenity and gratitude for "grace," a word and an ending which connect the novella with *The Holy Sinner*, Mann's last American work.

The original plan, the attempt to show how ambiguous and ambivalent Nature is and how she tricks one into believing that her disgusting, destructive manifestations are alive and beautiful, is seen in the episode of the pleasant scent, the source of which is a mound consisting of excrement, decaying plants, and the decomposed body of an animal.

Anna, who, unlike her mother, does not love nature—she is homely and has a clubfoot—also speaks of Nature's "propensity for the equivocal and for mystification" (110). To her mother's displeasure, she reduces nature, in her paintings, to abstract symbols and geometric figures. She also senses that her mother's "happy" erotic temptation has something to do with destruction (102).

Rosalie is a warm, lively, happy, and intelligent woman, one of Mann's most appealing characters. Her late love, which cannot be sanctioned by society, recalls Aschenbach's and Leverkühn's, but especially Mut's, who after many years without love "submissively and humbly" (54) loves a young foreign "servant." Mann treats her, as he treated Mut, with irony and sympathy. She is a "poor woman" (53) and a "good soul" (105). May is her favorite month, as it was Mann's. It brings her new energies and joy of life.

Ken Keaton is enthusiastic about Europe, its history, and its "atmosphere," and makes derogatory remarks about America, its bigotry, worship of success, its materialism, mediocrity, and poor educational system. In some respects he recalls Rudi Schwerdtfeger: He is pleasant, superficial, blond, and has only one kidney. One may be tempted to see in the story Mann's displeasure with America and its post-war relations with Germany or Europe, his conviction that the friendly feelings of the young country cannot help the charming old country or continent, which suffers from an incurable disease (nationalism?) or old age. But Ken is hardly a representative American, nor is Rosalie, as has been assumed, a symbol of Germany's middle class or Romanticism or Idealism. Any political interpretation of the novella seems far-fetched.

There is a new version of "Liebestod" in the novella. Rosalie and Ken embrace and kiss for the first and last time in the secret gallery of the castle "amid the decay, in the smell of death, in the grave" (132-133). Before her end, Rosalie feels that death has assumed for her the shape of love. But hers is not a Romantic yearning for union in death. She would prefer the love scene to take place in "kind Nature's lap, among the sweet breath of jasmine and alders," and she does not die gladly.

The two black swans, one of which angrily hisses when Rosalie eats some of the bread meant for them, have been seen as symbols of death, but Rosalie yearns to see the beautiful and majestic birds while she still is full of zest and love.

Cancer is a new entry in the long list of diseases "treated" in Mann's fiction. As in previous works, disease can raise the stature of a person. Anna's deformity "refines" her (12), and Rosalie, before her being stricken, had never known what love really is. In May 1952, Mann stated that Rosalie's ecstatic passion, which is not justified by the personality of the young man, may be a result of the irritation of the diseased organs.[11]

There is, according to Mann, irony in the fact that the "crassly clinical" story is told in the style of the classical novella.[12] The faded and sweetish metaphors and the oldish sentence structure form a sharp contrast to the naturalistic harshness in the description of the disease, and also to Anna's ultra-modern aesthetic views. The unrealistic discussions between mother and daughter about Nature, the soul, the heart, and the body, on the other hand, are intended, as Mann stated, to give the "painfully intimate story a certain stature."[13]

Briskly moving toward a climactic surprise ending, the story comes much closer to being a novella than many other stories of Mann. It has a lively and lovely protagonist and successfully evokes the atmosphere of a small Rococo castle on the Rhine, with its pond and the black swans, its mustiness, and shabby elegance. Clearly, the novella deserves a better reputation than it presently has.

CHAPTER 10

Essays

Of the twelve volumes of Mann's Collected Works published in 1960, four contain nonfiction. With few exceptions, they do not include his letters, nor the diaries which may only be published after 1975. Mann's essays start as early as about 1904 and end, perhaps climactically, in the year of his death with his essay on Schiller. They deal primarily with literature and politics. Some served as introductions to his own or other writers' books. Some were speeches written for inaugurations or anniversaries, and some were lectures for college audiences ("Goethe's *Faust*," "Goethe's *Werther*," "Introduction to *The Magic Mountain*," "The Art of the Novel").

Most of Mann's important literary essays deal with German writers. Some of these, such as Platen, Chamisso, Storm, and Fontane, are little known outside of Germany. Mann himself considered "On the Old Fontane" his best critical essay.[1] Once he stated that he would have been happier if he had written more about non-Germans such as Pascal, Diderot, and Keats.[2] No doubt, his essays on Pascal, Voltaire, Baudelaire, Conrad, and many other non-German writers would have been knowledgeable as well as lively. He did, however, publish a few essays about non-Germans, such as Tolstoy, Dostoevsky, Chekhov, Cervantes, and Shaw. The one on Chekhov is among his best.

Mann's whole essayistic œuvre springs, as he wrote in 1953,[3] from his admiration. And admiration, as this "ironic German" affirms in his essay on "Richard Wagner and the Ring" (*Essays*, 353), is "the best thing we have; the finest, happiest, most constructive, most indispensable." In many of Mann's essays one feels this "admiration, enthusiasm, absorption, devotion to something not himself, something much too large to be himself, yet something to which he feels most intimately allied." His admiration, however, is tempered and held in check by his sense of balance. On Nietzsche, Schopenhauer, and Wagner, whom he had once enthusiastically admired, he wrote no essays until he was past fifty and had gained a critical distance as well as a wider outlook on life and letters so that he could clearly distinguish the deficiencies of the masters, such as Nietzsche's pathological traits.

Mann's essays are based not only on his admiration, but also on wide reading, a prodigious memory, and his narrative power. While his fiction, particularly *The Magic Mountain, Joseph,* and *Doctor Faustus,* often embodies essayistic elements, his essays abound and excel in narrative passages. Some of the most striking biographical parts are the descriptions of Goethe's birth, of Schiller's burial, and of Tolstoy on his estate. Although Mann also consulted secondary sources, he is hardly ever pedantic. He often quotes from memory, and there are no footnotes or page references.

Like Mann's fictional work, his essays are often autobiographical, not only because he often tells about his own life and work but because he sometimes nearly transforms the person he writes about into a double of Thomas Mann, with the latter's experiences, problems, and thoughts. At times, an essay seems to be mostly concerned with himself. "Freud and the Future," for instance, might also be called "Mann and the Past."

Mann's properly autobiographical essays also throw light on his works. Chief among them are the "Account of My Stay in Paris" (1926) and "A Sketch of My Life," which he published in the *Neue Rundschau* in 1930. On the other hand, *The Story of a Novel* and other, much shorter comments about his own works illuminate his life.

Among the essays which played an important part in Mann's life and œuvre are the one on Frederick the Great and the *Reflections of a Non-Political Man.* The essay on "Frederick and the Great Coalition" was finished in December, 1914. It is one of Mann's best, but was wrongly branded by Western spokesmen as nationalistic and as a glorification of Germany's invasion of Belgium in World War I. While the Austrian Empress Maria Theresa, one of Frederick's adversaries, emerges from the essay as a healthy and likable person, Frederick is seen less as a super-hero than an implike, malicious, and sexless demon, an instrument and victim of destiny. He "had to do wrong and to lead a life against his own ideas and ideals." He was not allowed to be a philosopher of Enlightenment, but had to be a king. Years before the publication of the essay, Mann was planning a novel about the Prussian king.

Reflections of a Non-Political Man is in part a defense against the attacks that had been directed against the essay on Frederick. Among Mann's essays, the work occupies a special position for its length (over six hundred pages) and its nature. The book, which Mann began to write in November, 1915, and which he finished in March, 1918, is a rambling and confusing collection of essays. Some of the twelve chapters are entitled "About Virtue" and "Irony and Radicalism." Mann quotes, among others, Schiller, Nietzsche, Flaubert, Wagner, Dostoevsky, Tolstoy, Turgenev, Strindberg, Stifter, Ruskin, and Claudel. *Reflections* contains autobiography, protests, polemics, and literary criticism. Mann defends himself against the French pacifist Romain Rolland—whose novel *Jean-Christophe* he greatly admired—and, in many bitter pages, against his own brother Heinrich, who in an essay on Zola had accused him of nationalistic and militaristic opportunism. Mann compared his work on *Reflections*—which was written during "the most difficult years of his life" and supplanted all creative work proper, particularly on *The Magic Mountain*—with that of a galley slave.

The central idea of the book is that Germany stands for tradition, aristocracy, organic community of the folk, metaphysics, ethics, personality, music, freedom, culture, and is therefore irreconcilably opposed to politics, progress, individuality, democracy, literature, and civilization, which are represented by the Western countries. The bitterness of the tone partly stems from the fact that this alleged conflict between the German and Western character parallels Mann's favorite conflict between the artist and the burgher—one that was carried on in Mann's own mind and heart. Mann knew quite well that the future belonged to democracy and not to the authoritarian system which he so laboriously defended.

Mann once said that the best pages of the *Reflections* were those in which he had expressed his love. To these pages belong his comments on Paul Claudel's play *L'Annonce faite à Marie,* on Eichendorff's novella "Aus dem Leben eines Taugenichts," and on Pfitzner's opera *Palestrina.* Many "reflections" are restated with greater precision and objectivity in *The Magic Mountain.* In the novel, the *Zivilisationsliterat,* who is the villain of *Reflections,* is only gently derided and plays an appealing role, while the representative of conservatism and authoritarianism is much less likable and commits suicide. Already in 1922, in his speech on "The German Republic," Mann veers away from *Reflections* and champions democracy. He tries to make democracy more palatable to German nationalists by describing it as a synthesis of Novalis and Whitman. In the speech of 1922, as in *The Magic Mountain* of 1924, Germany is no longer represented as one of the two constituents of an irreconcilable polarity, but, on the contrary, as the country of the center, whose mission it is to mediate between East and West.

In the following years, Mann moved politically more and more to the left and finally saw in democratic socialism the future and salvation of mankind. His political essays and speeches became particularly numerous before and during World War II. During the war, from October 1940 on, he also addressed monthly broadcasts to Nazi Germany *(Listen, Germany!).* Some of his political, as well as non-political, essays, such as "War and Democracy" (1940), "How to Win the Peace" (1942), and "The War and the Future" (1944), were written in English. He sometimes felt that his many articles and speeches in defense of democracy were rather flat, and in March, 1952, he stated that his writing had been much more interesting and farther away from platitudes at the time of the "reactionary defiance" of his *Reflections.*[4]

In spite of the intellectual, narrative, and stylistic brilliance of many essays, Mann's essayistic oeuvre stands in the shadow of his towering fiction. Some essays announce or paraphrase certain novels. *Reflections* (1918), "Goethe and Tolstoy" (1922), and the "Experiences of the Occult" (1924) belong to *The Magic Mountain;* "Kleist's *Amphitryon*" (1926), "Lessing" (1929), "Sufferings and Greatness of Richard Wagner" (1933), and "Freud and the Future" (1936) to *Joseph;* "Germany and the Germans" (1945), "Dostoevsky Within Limits" (1946), and "Nietzsche's Philosophy in the Light of Contemporary Events" (1947) to *Doctor Faustus.* Often when Mann expresses the same idea in a novel and an essay, the formulation in his fiction has more keenness and stylistic finesse.

CHAPTER 11

Letters

A LARGE and important part of Mann's nonfictional work is formed by his correspondence. Although eight volumes of his letters have already been published, these only represent a fragment, perhaps not even one third, of his epistolary activity. It is assumed that he wrote about 20,000 letters. Many of these, however, have been lost, such as most of his letters to his wife, the early letters to his children, many of those to S. Fischer—his publisher—to Hans Reisiger, Emil Preetorius, and Bruno Frank. The hundreds of correspondents include, understandably, some very great names, such as Hofmannsthal, Schnitzler, Freud, Gide, Einstein, Hauptmann, and Hesse. While he lived in the United States, his correspondence increased considerably. He wrote about four hundred letters to Agnes Meyer, wife of the publisher of the *Washington Post;* and these letters, according to Erika Mann, who edited a great part of her father's correspondence, form a story of sorts.[1]

Since Mann often speaks quite freely about his works, his plans, his doubts, and his hopes concerning them, even when writing to relative strangers, his correspondence constitutes a valuable commentary on his creative work. In addition, it throws light on his life, his time, and many of his contemporaries. One sees him as a bridegroom, a father, a colleague, a friend, a brother, a fighter, a helper, and a seeker of information.

One of the letters that have become famous is that written in 1937 and addressed to the Dean of the Philosophical Faculty of the University of Bonn after the announcement that Mann's honorary doctorate had been taken from him. Mann wrote to the Dean that he had always felt at home in the intellectual traditions of his nation, that he was better suited to represent them than to become a martyr for them, but that he could not remain silent since his country was threatening the whole world with war, a war from which it could never rise again. And the exile, who had remained silent during the first years of the Third Reich because he wanted to retain his German audience, concluded his letter with a sentence which heralded Zeitblom's final comments in *Doctor Faustus:* "God help our darkened and desecrated country and teach it to make its peace with the world and with itself."

In his letters Mann is hardly ever intimate or emotional. The prevailing tone is that of polite friendliness. Even his anger or grief is expressed in measured words. Although he usually wrote his letters in the (for him) less productive hours of the afternoon, while the mornings were reserved for his creative work, one gets the impression that the letters, too, are meant to be fit for print. Mann abhorred carelessness in thought and form, and even his most "informal" notes have a polished look.

In many letters, he discusses the plans, articles, and books of strangers with a view toward encouraging or enlightening them. He read many manuscripts and books sent to him, and his judgments are often overly kind. Many letters also show his active desire to help people in distress, particularly after Hitler's rise to power. Because of the size, social importance, intellectual depth, and formal perfection of his correspondence, Mann is without doubt one of the great letter-writers of all time.

CHAPTER 12

Conclusion

IN ONE respect at least, Thomas Mann was as "lonely" as he often claimed to be. He did not join any literary movement, nor did he start one. He stood alone, like his friend Hermann Hesse. But he drew greatly and gratefully upon the literary wealth of the past. Quite a few German, French, Russian, English, and Scandinavian writers inspired him, in addition to the Bible, the *Odyssey*, Indian legends, and Babylonian tales.

He was steeped in literary tradition, but his family novel, his novel of education, his picaresque novel, and his novellas strike a new and personal tone. He invigorated the novel, as Joyce, Proust, Kafka, and the authors of the "nouveau roman" had done or were to do. He parodied traditional forms, but also rejuvenated them with love, playfulness, sophistication, and humor.

He took subject matter and literary forms from classical and non-classical antiquity, from the Middle Ages, the sixteenth, seventeenth, eighteenth, and nineteenth centuries; and yet he was timely and modern. He thought of himself as being, like André Gide, a "bold conservative" or a "cautious radical." He learned from many German Romantic as well as Realistic writers of the nineteenth century and constantly praised such novelists as Keller, Stifter, Storm, and particularly Fontane; but compared to him they almost look parochial, dusty, and dull. He raised the German novel, which, in the nineteenth century, was hardly known outside of Germany, to a level commanding world-wide attention.

As a genuine Realist, he valued careful documentation, keen observation, and precise description. And, like an author of conventional novels, he was also concerned with plot and character. But the realism and the traditional narrative of his fiction are deepened by ideas, symbols, allusions, myths, and penetrating psychology. His intellectual range and sharpness are often admirable. What he says of Wagner applies to himself: He celebrates a "feast of associations" and creates a "world of profound and brilliant allusions." And again, as in Wagner, in him the "Naturalism of the nineteenth century is consecrated through the myth" (*Essays,* 367, 270). His mythology, on the other hand, is coupled with a searching and revealing psychology, which he acquired from Nietzsche and Freud.

The encyclopedic passages of his fiction are not mere patchwork of his wide reading, but are organically interwoven with the rest of the novels. His extensive and varied knowledge and his serious thoughts blend gracefully with his wit and humor. He is one of the greatest German humorists and, particularly in his last years, wanted to be considered primarily as such.[1]

His artistry shines perhaps most brightly in his style. Because of the vastness of his verbal range, the ease and vigor of his language, the ability to construct delightfully, sometimes irritatingly, intricate and long yet always lucid sentences, he is one of the very great German stylists, a worthy disciple and successor of Goethe and Nietzsche.

As he himself stated, he only wrote what was natural to him. He did not write to follow or set a trend, to please a clique or the fashion of the day, or to shock the general public. And yet his work has been enormously successful during and after his life, with the general reader as well as with the sophisticated critics. His novels are full of artful repetitions. But he did not repeat himself by following a successful novel with a similar one. He rather experimented with a new art form or a new idea, even though this involved a greater effort. While he was writing a work, he often did not believe in its eventual success.

His long life was one of hard and incessant work. Though not all of his creations are masterpieces, none is carelessly done. He wanted to be an entertainer, but also a teacher and a servant of the human cause, though he sometimes had his doubts about the seriousness, morality, and usefulness of art.

His ambiguities, his irony, parody, and coldness, his fascination with nihilism notwithstanding, there is, as he wrote to a French critic[2] in April, 1954, a certain basic and constructive unity and sincerity in his work, a desire not to bewilder, but to

[158]

satisfy his readers, or, as Hesse once said, "a great heart, loyalty, a sense of responsibility, and a capacity for affection."[3] In spite of the coldness of his artist figures, he extends his "sympathy" toward all men and feels "friendliness" for life. His humanism is fully aware of man's weakness and wickedness; yet, it is also reverent toward man's spirit and his possibilities. Generally it can be said that his development went from the pessimistic and ironic stress on eternal opposites, such as that between spirit and life, to the hopeful advocacy of mediation, reconciliation, and unity.

Mann's success has ben universal because he is superb as an observer, a craftsman, a creator, a thinker, and a humorist. He embodies or symbolizes a vast intellectual and artistic tradition and, yet, at the same time, he is sensitive to the problems and possibilities of the present and the future. He does not hide his views in obscure language, or a private symbolism, or in an Olympian aloofness. His brilliance is one that not only dazzles, but also enlightens.

In December, 1952, he contended that it had been his endeavor, throughout his life, to contribute to the great cultural heritage of the West and to spread truth and joy among his fellow men.[4] Millions of readers all over the world are grateful witnesses that the patrician-artist from Lübeck succeeded magnificently in this endeavor.

Notes and References

Abbreviations used are *GF* for Thomas Mann, *Gesammelte Werke in zwölf Bänden* (Frankfurt, 1960); *MB II* for Thomas Mann, *Briefe 1937-1947* (Frankfurt, 1963); *MB III* for Thomas Mann, *Briefe 1948-1955 und Nachlese* (Frankfurt, 1965).

Chapter One

1. *GF*, X, 872.

Chapter Three

1. HERMANN J. WEIGAND, *Thomas Mann's Novel "Der Zauberberg"* (New York: Appleton-Century, 1933), p. 142.
2. "Time-romance," p. 685, is a misleading translation.
3. HENRY HATFIELD, *Thomas Mann*, rev. ed. (Norfolk, Conn.: New Directions, 1962), p. 87.
4. Curiously enough, another young man—the central figure of a novel that appeared only a few years before *The Magic Mountain* —equally delights in the moments when, for his feeling, time has stopped its inexorable flow: Marcel in Proust's *Remembrance of Things Past*.
5. The Czech diacritical mark on the *c* is probably correct, not the cedilla used by Mann. Except for the ending *-ek*, the name, when pronounced, is the same as that of the Hungarian writer.

Chapter Four

1. *MB II*, 247.

Chapter Five

1. In *The Stature of Thomas Mann*, ed. Charles Neider (New York, 1947), p. 188.

Chapter Six

1. In spite of the *Story of a Novel* (30-31), this is not quite the same day on which Mann started *Doctor Faustus* (May 23, 1943).
2. ERICH KAHLER, "The Devil Secularized," in *Thomas Mann: A*

Collection of Critical Essays, ed. Henry Hatfield (Englewood, N. J.: Prentice-Hall, 1964), p. 109.

3. Since Zeitblom and Mann are silent on this point and Adrian obviously could not have lived on his compositions and their performances, the reader must assume that he has been supported throughout his life by his family. How this agrees with his pride is another question.

4. *MB III,* 22.

5. *MB III,* 38.

Chapter Seven

1. *MB III,* 33.

2. *MB III,* 251.

3. *MB III,* 245.

4. *MB III,* 201, 210.

5. *MB III,* 345.

Chapter Eight

1. *MB III,* 225.

2. THOMAS MANN, *Nachlese. Prosa 1951-1955* (Frankfurt, 1956), p. 194; Robert B. Heilman, "Variations on Picaresque *(Felix Krull),*" *Sewanee Review,* LXVI (1958), 547-577; Oskar Seidlin, "Pacaresque Elements in Thomas Mann's Work," *Modern Language Quarterly,* XII (1951), 183-200.

3. *MB III,* 357.

Chapter Nine

1. ERICH HELLER, *The Ironic German: A Study of Thomas Mann* (Boston, 1958), pp. 78, 84.

2. Aschenbach's "love of the ocean" in the standard English translation (401) should, therefore, read "love of the sea."

3. JOACHIM SEYPPEL, "Adel des Geistes: Thomas Mann und August von Platen," *Deutsche Vierteljahrsschrift für Literaturwissenschaft und Geistesgeschichte,* XXXIII (1959), 565-573; Werner Vordtriede, "Richard Wagners Tod in Venedig," *Euphorion,* LII (1959), 386.

4. ERWIN ROHDE, *Psyche* (Tübingen, 1910), II, 46.

5. G. M. A. GRUBE, *The Drama of Euripides* (London, 1961), p. 419.

6. Repeatedly he is called "solitary" or "lonely" (395, 413, 416, 422, twice on 425, twice on 427; missing in the translation on 426 and 429).

7. *MB II,* 198.

8. *MB II,* 152.

9. In Mann's works, the arms seem to be singled out for their beauty and arouse love or desire more often than any other part of the human body. The most noteworthy examples are Clavdia's, Mut's, Esmeralda's, Zouzou's, and Ken Keaton's arms. Pharao's daughter is also particularly fascinated by the arms of a Jewish servant, who eventually sires Moses.

10. Both Rosalie and Felix, incidentally, are born in May, live in the Rhineland, and see in love a "miracle" (132).

11. *MB III*, 255.

12. *GF*, XI, 530.

13. *Ibid.*

Chapter Ten

1. *MB III*, 190.
2. *GF*, IX, 756.
3. *MB III*, 315.
4. *MB III*, 248.

Chapter Eleven

1. *MB II*, 6.

Chapter Twelve

1. *MB III*, 152.
2. *Neue Rundschau*, LXXVII (1966), 228.
3. Erika Mann, *The Last Year* (London, 1958), p. 27.
4. *MB III*, 281.

Selected Bibliography

BIBLIOGRAPHIES

BÜRGIN, HANS. *Das Werk Thomas Manns.* Frankfurt: S. Fischer, 1959. (Includes references to almost everything written by Thomas Mann.)

JONAS, KLAUS W. *Fifty Years of Thomas Mann Studies.* Minneapolis: University of Minnesota Press, 1955. (Rather comprehensive and reliable listing of books and articles written on Thomas Mann in German, English, and other languages between 1902 and 1951; also has a checklist of Mann's principal publications.)

JONAS, KLAUS W. and JONAS, ILSEDORE B. *Thomas Mann Studies: Volume II.* Philadelphia: University of Pennsylvania Press, 1967. (Contains a chapter on all of Mann's manuscripts.)

MANN'S WORKS IN GERMAN

Mann's works were published almost exclusively by S. Fischer (Berlin, then Vienna, then Stockholm, and now Frankfurt), and for some time by the Bermann-Fischer Verlag.

A. COLLECTED WORKS

Gesammelte Werke. In single volumes. Berlin, 1922-1935.

Gesammelte Werke in zehn Bänden. Berlin, 1925.

Stockholmer Gesamtausgabe der Werke. In single volumes. Stockholm, 1938; Amsterdam, 1948; Vienna, 1949; Frankfurt, 1950- . Much more complete than the above items, but marred by many misprints.

Gesammelte Werke in zwölf Bänden. Berlin: Aufbau-Verlag, 1955. The standard edition in Eastern Germany, smaller than its Western counterpart.

Gesammelte Werke in zwölf Bänden. Frankfurt, 1960. The most complete and most reliable edition, with useful bibliographical notes.

B. FIRST EDITIONS

a. Novels

Buddenbrooks: Verfall einer Familie. Berlin, 1901.

Königliche Hoheit. Berlin, 1909.

Der Zauberberg. Berlin, 1924.
Die Geschichten Jaakobs. Berlin, 1933. (First volume of the tetralogy *Joseph und seine Brüder.*) ..
Der junge Joseph. Berlin, 1934. (Second volume of the tetralogy.)
Joseph in Agypten. Vienna, 1936. (Third volume of the tetralogy.)
Lotte in Weimar. Stockholm, 1939.
Joseph, der Ernährer. Stockholm, 1943. (Fourth volume of the tetralogy.)
Doktor Faustus. Stockholm, 1947.
Der Erwählte. Frankfurt, 1951.
Bekenntnisse des Hochstaplers Felix Krull: Der Memoiren erster Teil. Frankfurt, 1954.

b. Stories

Der kleine Herr Friedemann. Berlin, 1898. (Six novellas.)
Tristan. Berlin, 1903. (Six novellas including "Tonio Kröger.")
Der Tod in Venedig. Munich, 1912.
Das Wunderkind. Berlin, 1914. (Five novellas.)
Herr und Hund. Gesang vom Kindchen. Zwei Idyllen. Berlin, 1919.
Wälsungenblut. Munich, 1921.
Unordnung und frühes Leid. Berlin, 1926.
Mario und der Zauberer. Berlin, 1930.
Die vertauschten Köpfe. Stockholm, 1940.
Das Gesetz. Stockholm, 1944.
Die Betrogene. Frankfurt, 1953.

c. Theater

Fiorenza. Berlin, 1906.

d. Critical and Political Writings

Friedrich und die große Koalition. Berlin, 1915.
Betrachtungen eines Unpolitischen. Berlin, 1918.
Rede und Antwort. Berlin, 1922. (Collection of essays.)
Goethe und Tolstoi. Aachen, 1923.
Von deutscher Republik. Berlin, 1923.
Bemühungen. Berlin, 1925. (Collection of essays.)
Pariser Rechenschaft. Berlin, 1926.
Die Forderung des Tages. Berlin, 1930. (Collection of essays.)
Leiden und Größe der Meister. Berlin, 1935. (Six essays, later incorporated in *Adel des Geistes.*)
Freud und die Zukunft. Vienna, 1936.
Ein Briefwechsel. Zurich, 1937.
Achtung, Europa! Stockholm, 1938.
Deutsche Hörer. Stockholm, 1942. (Radio broadcasts.)

Selected Bibliography

Adel des Geistes. Stockholm, 1945. (Sixteen of the most important essays.)
Neue Studien. Stockholm, 1948.
Die Entstehung des "Doktor Faustus." Amsterdam, 1949.
Altes und Neues. Frankfurt, 1953. (Small items from "five decades.")
Versuch über Schiller. Frankfurt, 1955.
Nachlese. Prosa 1951-1955. Frankfurt, 1956.
Reden und Aufsätze I. Frankfurt, 1965.
Reden und Aufsätze II. Frankfurt, 1965.

e. Letters

KANTOROWICZ, ALFRED. *Heinrich und Thomas Mann: Die persönlichen, literarischen und weltanschaulichen Beziehungen der Brüder.* Berlin, 1956. (Contains many letters by Thomas Mann to his brother Heinrich.)
MANN, THOMAS. *Briefe an Paul Amann, 1915-1952,* ed. Herbert Wegener. Lübeck: Max Schmidt-Römhild, 1959.
Thomas Mann an Ernst Bertram: Briefe aus den Jahren 1910-1955, ed. Inge Jens. Pfullingen: Neske, 1960.
Thomas Mann–Karl Kerényi. Gespräch in Briefen. Zurich: Atlantis, 1960.
Mann, Thomas. Briefe 1899-1936, ed. Erika Mann. Frankfurt, 1961.
Thomas Mann–Robert Faesi. Briefwechsel, ed. Robert Faesi. Zurich: Atlantis, 1962.
MANN, THOMAS. *Briefe 1937-1947,* ed. Erika Mann. Frankfurt, 1963.
MANN, THOMAS. *Briefe 1948-1955 und Nachlese,* ed. Erika Mann. Frankfurt, 1965.

MANN'S WORKS IN ENGLISH

All are published by Alfred A. Knopf, New York, unless otherwise stated. The translator is Helen T. Lowe-Porter, unless otherwise indicated.

Royal Highness: A Novel of German Court Life. Tr. A. Cecil Curtis. 1916. (Title in German: *Königliche Hoheit.*)
Buddenbrooks. 1924.
Death in Venice. Tr. Kenneth Burke. 1925. (Title in German: "Der Tod in Venedig." Also contains "Tristan" and "Tonio Kröger.")
The Magic Mountain. Two vols. 1927. (In German: *Der Zauberberg.*) In one volume, 1928.
Past Masters and Other Papers. 1933.

Joseph and His Brothers: I. *Joseph and His Brothers.* 1934. (In German *Die Geschichten Jaakobs*); II, *Young Joseph.* 1935. (*Der junge Joseph*); III. *Joseph in Egypt.* 1938. (*Joseph in Agypten*); IV. *Joseph the Provider.* 1944. (*Joseph, der Ernährer*). The complete work in one volume, 1948.

Stories of Three Decades. 1936.

The Beloved Returns. 1940. (German title: *Lotte in Weimar.*)

The Transposed Heads. 1941. (German title: *Die vertauschten Köpfe.*)

Order of the Day: Political Essays and Speeches of Two Decades. Tr. Helen T. Lowe-Porter, Agnes E. Meyer, and Eric Sutton. 1942.

The Tables of the Law. 1945. (German title: *Das Gesetz.*)

Essays of Three Decades. 1947. (German title: *Adel des Geistes.*)

Doctor Faustus: The Life of the German Composer Adrian Leverkühn as Told by a Friend. 1948.

The Thomas Mann Reader. Selected, edited, and with introductions by Joseph Warner Angell. New York: Grosset & Dunlap, 1950.

The Holy Sinner. 1951. (German title: *Der Erwählte.*)

The Black Swan. Tr. Willard R. Trask. 1954. (German title: *Die Betrogene.*)

Confessions of Felix Krull, Confidence Man: The Early Years. Tr. Denver Lindley, 1955.

Last Essays. Tr. Richard and Clara Winston, and Tania and James Stern. 1959.

Letters to Paul Amann. Tr. Richard and Clara Winston. Middletown, Conn.: Wesleyan University Press, 1960.

A Sketch of My Life. 1960. (German title: *Lebensabriß.*)

The Story of a Novel: The Genesis of "Doctor Faustus." Tr. Richard and Clara Winston. 1961.

SECONDARY SOURCES

1. *Books*

ALTENBERG, PAUL. *Die Romane Thomas Manns: Versuch einer Deutung.* Bad Homburg: Gentner, 1961.

BAUER, ARNOLD. *Thomas Mann.* Berlin: Colloquium-Verlag, 1960.

BAUMGART, REINHARD. *Das Ironische und die Ironie in den Werken Thomas Manns.* Munich: Hanser, 1964.

BERENDSOHN, WALTER A. *Thomas Mann: Künstler und Kämpfer in bewegter Zeit.* Lübeck: Schmidt-Römhild, 1965.

BERGSTEN, GUNILLA. *Thomas Manns "Doktor Faustus": Untersuchungen zu den Quellen und zur Struktur des Romans.* Stockholm: Svenska Bokförlaget, 1963.

Selected Bibliography

BLUME, BERNARD. *Thomas Mann und Goethe.* Bern: Francke, 1949.
(A sound and sensitive study.)

BRENNAN, JOSEPH GERARD. *Thomas Mann's World.* New York:
Columbia University Press, 1942. (Concentrates on the earlier
works and the relation between art, disease, and life.)

BÜRGIN, HANS and HANS-OTTO MAYER. *Thomas Mann: Eine
Chronik seines Lebens.* Frankfurt: S. Fischer, 1965. (Very
useful and reliable chronicle with many quotations.)

DIERSEN, INGE. *Untersuchungen zu Thomas Mann: Die Bedeutung
der Künstlerdarstellung für die Entwicklung des Realismus in
seinem erzählerischen Werk.* Berlin: Rütten und Loening, 1959.

EICHNER, HANS. *Thomas Mann: Eine Einführung in sein Werk.*
Bern: Francke, 1961.

ELOESSER, ARTHUR. *Thomas Mann: Sein Leben und sein Werk.*
Berlin: S. Fischer, 1925.

FAESI, ROBERT. *Thomas Mann, ein Meister der Erzählkunst.* Zurich:
Atlantis, 1955.

FEUERLICHT, IGNACE. *Thomas Mann und die Grenzen des Ich.*
Heidelberg: Winter, 1966.

FLINKER, KARL, ed. *Hommage de la France à Thomas Mann à l'occasion de son quatre-vingtième anniversaire.* Paris: Editions
Flinker, 1955. (French official as well as critical tributes to the
octogenarian.)

FLINKER, MARTIN. *Thomas Manns politische Betrachtungen im
Lichte der heutigen Zeit.* 's-Gravenhage: Mouton, 1959.

FOUGÈRE, JEAN. *Thomas Mann ou la Séduction de la mort.* Paris:
Editions du Pavois, 1947.

HAMBURGER, KÄTE. *Thomas Mann und die Romantik: Eine pro-
blemgeschichtliche Studie.* Berlin: Junker und Dünnhaupt,
1932.

————. *Thomas Manns Roman "Joseph und seine Brüder": Eine
Einführung.* Stockholm: Bermann-Fischer, 1945.

————. *Der Humor bei Thomas Mann: Zum Joseph-Roman.* Munich: Nymphenburger Verlagsbuchhandlung, 1965.

HATFIELD, HENRY. *Thomas Mann.* Revised edition. Norfolk, Conn.:
New Directions, 1962.

HATFIELD, HENRY, ed. *Thomas Mann: A Collection of Critical Essays.* Englewood, N. J.: Prentice-Hall, 1964 (Twelve valuable
essays by American, British, and German writers, including Elizabeth M. Wilkinson's on "Tonio Kröger" and Erich
Kahler's on "The Devil Secularized.")

HELLER, ERICH. *The Ironic German: A Study of Thomas Mann.*
Boston: Little, Brown & Company, 1958. (Often brilliant and
provocative.)

HELLERSBERG-WENDRINER, ANNA. *Mystik der Gottesferne: Eine Interpretation Thomas Manns.* Bern: Francke, 1960.

HIRSCHBACH, FRANK DONALD. *The Arrow and the Lyre: A Study of the Role of Love in the Works of Thomas Mann.* The Hague: Nijhoff, 1955.

KAUFMANN, FRITZ. *Thomas Mann: The World as Will and Representation.* Boston: Beacon Press, 1957. (Erudite investigation of the philosophical foundations and implications of Mann's works.)

KOOPMANN, HELMUT. *Die Entwicklung des intellektualen Romans bei Thomas Mann: Untersuchungen zur Struktur von "Buddenbrooks," "Königliche Hoheit" und "Der Zauberberg."* Bonn: Bouvier, 1962.

LEHNERT, HERBERT. *Thomas Mann: Fiktion, Mythos, Religion.* Stuttgart: Kohlhammer, 1965.

LESSER, JONAS. *Thomas Mann in der Epoche seiner Vollendung.* Munich: Desch, 1952.

LINDSAY, MARTIN. *Thomas Mann.* Oxford: Basil Blackwell, 1954. (Studies certain recurrent themes.)

LION, FERDINAND. *Thomas Mann: Leben und Werk.* Revised edition. Zurich: Oprecht, 1955.

LUKÁCS, GEORG. *Thomas Mann.* Fifth edition. Berlin: Aufbau-Verlag, 1957. (Most important Marxist study of Mann.)

MANN, ERIKA. *The Last Year of Thomas Mann.* Tr. Richard Graves. New York: Farrar, Strauss, & Cudahy, 1958. (A moving factual account.)

MANN, MONIKA. *Past and Present,* tr. F. F. Reid and Ruth Hein. New York: St. Martin's Press, 1960.

MANN, VIKTOR. *Wir waren fünf: Bildnis der Familie Mann.* Konstanz: Südverlag, 1949.

MAYER, HANS. *Thomas Mann: Werk und Entwicklung.* Berlin: Volk und Welt, 1950.

NEIDER, CHARLES, ed. *The Stature of Thomas Mann.* New York: New Directions, 1947. (An uneven anthology of sixty essays, many in translation, some not published elsewhere.)

SAGAVE, PIERRE-PAUL. *Réalité sociale et idéologie religieuse dans les romans de Thomas Mann.* Paris: Belles Lettres, 1954.

SCHRÖTER, KLAUS. *Thomas Mann in Selbstzeugnissen und Bilddokumenten.* Hamburg: Rowohlt, 1964. (Biography in paperback. Many photographs and excerpts from autobiographical writings.)

Sinn und Form. Sonderheft Thomas Mann, 1965, ed. Hans Bunge. (Special issue of the East German periodical; contains documents of the Mann family, essays on Mann, and some letters.)

Selected Bibliography

SONTHEIMER, KURT. *Thomas Mann und die Deutschen.* Munich: Nymphenburger Verlagsbuchhandlung, 1961. (A sound analysis of Mann's political views.)

STRESAU, HERMANN. *Thomas Mann und sein Werk.* Frankfurt: S. Fischer, 1963.

THOMAS, RICHARD H. *Thomas Mann: The Mediation of Art.* Oxford: Clarendon Press, 1956.

WEIGAND, HERMANN JOHN. *Thomas Mann's Novel "Der Zauberberg."* New York: Appleton-Century, 1933.

WEISS, WALTER. *Thomas Manns Kunst der sprachlichen und thematischen Integration.* Düsseldorf: Schwann, 1964. (Good chapter on "Mario and the Magician.")

WENZEL, GEORG, ed. *Vollendung und Größe Thomas Manns: Beiträge zu Werk und Persönlichkeit des Dichters.* Halle: Sprache und Literatur, 1962. (Twenty essays, mostly new. Some letters by Mann.)

WHITE, ANDREW. *Thomas Mann.* Edinburgh: Oliver and Boyd, 1965. (Brief; contains a useful survey of Mann's essays and of writings about him.)

WOLFF, HANS M. *Thomas Mann.* Bern: Francke, 1957.

2. Articles

BEHARRIELL, FREDERICK J. "Psychology in the Early Works of Thomas Mann." *PMLA,* LXXVII (1962), 149-155.

BLISSETT, WILLIAM. "Thomas Mann: The Last Wagnerite." *Germanic Review,* XXXV (1960), 50-76.

BURKHARDT, ARTHUR. "Thomas Mann's Treatment of the Marked Man." *PMLA,* XLIII (1928), 561-568.

CASSIRER, ERNST. "Thomas Manns Goethebild: Eine Studie über *Lotte in Weimar.*" *Germanic Review,* XX (1945), 166-194.

EXNER, RICHARD. "Zur Essayistik Thomas Manns." *Germanisch-romanische Monatsschrift,* XII (1962), 51-78.

GRONICKA, ANDRÉ VON. "Myth plus Psychology: A Style Analysis of 'Death in Venice'." *Germanic Review,* XXXI (1956), 191-205.

HELLER, PETER. "Thomas Mann's Conception of the Creative Writer." *PMLA,* LXIX (1954), 763-796.

HUNT, JOEL A. "The Stylistics of a Foreign Language: Thomas Mann's Use of French." *Germanic Review,* XXXII (1957), 19-34.

LÄMMERT, EBERHARD. "Thomas Mann: *Buddenbrooks.*" *Der deutsche Roman,* II, ed. Benno von Wiese. Düsseldorf: Bagel, 1963, pp. 190-233. (Particularly good on the structure of *Buddenbrooks.*)

LEHNERT, HERBERT. "Thomas Mann in Exile, 1933-1938." *Germanic Review*, XXXVII (1963), 277-294.

———. "Thomas Mann in Princeton." *Germanic Review*, XXXIX (1964), 15-32.

———. "Thomas Mann's Early Interest in Myth and Erwin Rohde's *Psyche*." *PMLA*, LXXIX (1964), 297-304.

MAUTNER, FRANZ H. "Die griechischen Anklänge in Thomas Manns "Tod in Venedig." *Monatshefte*, XLIV (1952), 20-26.

MICHAEL, WOLFGANG. "Stoff und Idee im 'Tod in Venedig'." *Deutsche Vierteljahrsschrift für Literaturwissenschaft und Geistesgeschichte*, XXXIII (1959), 13-19.

MÜLLER, JOACHIM. "Thomas Manns *Doktor Faustus*: Grundthematik und Motivgefüge." *Euphorion*, LIX (1961), 262-280.

REY, WILLIAM H. "Rechtfertigung der Liebe in Thomas Manns Erzählung *Die Betrogene*." *Deutsche Vierteljahrsschrift für Literaturwissenschaft und Geistesgeschichte*, XXXIV (1960), 428-448.

SCHERRER, PAUL. "Bruchstücke der *Buddenbrooks*-Urhandschrift und Zeugnisse zu ihrer Entstehung, 1897-1901." *Neue Rundschau*, LXIX (1958), 258-291.

SCHOOLFIELD, GEORGE C. "Thomas Mann's *Die Betrogene*." *Germanic Review*, XXXVIII (1963), 91-120.

SCHULTZ, SIEGFRIED A. "*Die vertauschten Köpfe*: Thomas Manns indische Travestie." *Euphorion*, LVII (1963), 245-271.

SEIDLIN, OSCAR. "Picaresque Elements in Thomas Mann's Work." *Modern Language Quarterly*, XII (1951), 183-200.

STACKMANN, KARL. "*Der Erwählte*: Thomas Manns Mittelalter-Parodie." *Euphorion*, LIII (1959), 61-74.

WEIGAND, HERMANN J. "Thomas Mann's Gregorius." *Germanic Review*, XXVII (1952), 10-30, 83-93.

WIESE, BENNO VON. "Thomas Mann: 'Der Tod in Venedig' " in *Die deutsche Novelle von Goethe bis Kafka*, I. Düsseldorf: Bagel, 1956, 304-324.

WYSLING, HANS. "Die Technik der Montage: Zu Thomas Manns *Erwählten*." *Euphorion*, LVII (1963), 156-199.

———. "Aschenbachs Werke: Archivalische Untersuchungen an einem Thomas Mann-Satz." *Euphorion*, LIX (1965), 272-314.

Index

1. NAMES

Index

2. THOMAS MANN'S WORKS

Index

3. OTHER WORKS

DATE DUE